North Country Almanac

Journal of the Adirondack Seasons

...Mother Earth, after violent contraction, gave birth to twins which we have named Flora and Fauna.

By

Robert F. Hall

Purple Mountain Press
Fleischmanns, New York

First Edition, 1990
published by
Purple Mountain Press, Ltd.
Main Street
Fleischmanns, New York 12430

Copyright © 1990 by Robert F. Hall

All rights reserved. No part of this publication may be reproduced or transmitted in any form without permission in writing from the publisher, except to quote brief passages in connection with a review written for inclusion in a magazine, newspaper or broadcast.

ISBN: 0-935796-18-5

Cover photograph by Bill Healy

Printed in the United States of America

Acknowledgements

For the complicated process of publication, I am indebted to my daughter Molly Hall Miller for editing this manuscript and acting as my literary agent, and to Suzanne Perley for composition and graphic design. For permission to reprint these essays, I thank the publishers of the publications in which they appeared: *The Valley News* of Elizabethtown, the *Plattsburgh Press Republican*, the *Adirondack Journal*, the *Warrensburg-Lake George News*, the *Conservationist* magazine, and *The New York Times*.

Robert F. Hall

CONTENTS

Dedicated to the Memory of Barney Fowler
Foreword

SPRING

Early Spring	15
The Black Fly and the Dandelion	17
The Season's First Butterfly	19
An Early Bird - The Phoebe	20
The Water Strider	22
The Adirondack Guide	23
The Great Blue Heron	24
The Return of the Brown-Headed Cowbirds	25
Daffodil Time	27
Backpacking in May, Blue Mountain Lake, N.Y.	28
The Miracle of Mutation	33
Seasons	35
Meet the Hawthorn	37
An Apology for Anthropods	39

SUMMER

Observing Nature	42
An Answer to the Chickadee Puzzle	43
Remembering Isaak Walton	44
Eastward in Eden	46
Nature and Sex	47
Bird Symphony	49
The Hedgerow, Nature's Workshop	50
The Pugnacious Ruby Throat	51
The Media and the Environment	53
Strange Animals that Thrive on Poison	56
The Spiderwort Alert	58
Midsummer Review	59

FALL

A Labor Day Reverie	62
This is Bear Season	63
Chicadees	65
The Bugs of Autumn	67
Salute to the Apple	68
The Digger Wasp: Life Without Mother Love	70
The Monarch Miracle	71
Tamarack	73
The First Frost	73
Love of Bare November Days	75
Questions Without Answers	76
Driven by Some Enchantment	77
Animal Intelligence	81
Pain	83
The Wooly Bear	84
An Autumn Walk in the Woods	85

THE BETWIXT AND BETWEEN SEASON

The Betwixt and Between Season	88

WINTER

Prescription for Cabin Fever I	94
Prescription for Cabin Fever II	96
An Unmistakable Symptom	97
A Bad Guest	96
The January Thaw	99
The Mourning Dove	100
The Grosbeaks	102
About Birch, Rabbits and Forsythia	104
Some Benefits of Snow	105
Creation and Diversity	106

Our White Pine Forests	109
The First Frost	110
Continuity, Predictability	112
Northern Lights	113
Memorial to the Dodo Bird	114

NOTES ON NATURE WRITING AND NATURE WRITERS

The Craft of Outdoor Writing	118
Virgil	120
Sir Francis Bacon	120
Reverend Gilbert White	121
Ralph Waldo Emerson	121
Henry David Thoreau	122
William Bartram	123
John Burroughs	123
John Muir	123
Ernest Thompson Seton	124
Aldo Leopold	124
Rachel Carson	125
Henry Beston	126
Edwin Way Teale	127
Joseph Wood Krutch	127
William Chapman White	128
E.B. White	128
Stephen Jay Gould	129
Dr. Lewis Thomas	131
DiNunzio and Lacy	132
Other Almanacs	133

Dedicated to the memory of Barney Fowler

He was a friend of the outdoors, of outdoor sports, of nature, of environmental protection, of wildlife, of rural life and rural people, of local history, of individual liberty, of local organizations and their activities.

He was implacably against big government, big business, civil servants who misused government property, speeding truck drivers, drug dealers, and misguided office holders who would cut in half the number of forest rangers.

During his twenty years as a columnist for the *Albany Times Union* he drove his car tirelessly north of Albany collecting the news of these areas and passing it on to his readers with frank comment that made us completely aware of how such events fitted into this code of his.

Barney Fowler seemed to know thousands of people, and all of them called him by his first name. He was an honorary member of every fish and game club in the state and was a welcome guest at any environmental group meeting.

He might show up at almost any gathering. He was in Essex County for the dedication of the fish ladder, for sailboat races, and for hearings on the visitor interpretation center, for example.

Barney also knew how to use the telephone. His friends were never surprised at a call at an ungodly hour from Barney seeking information on a happening of which he surmised they had special knowledge.

It was never clear where he got all the energy. In addition to his six columns a week, he put together three books. He called them the *Adirondack Albums* and one is indeed fortunate who owns all three. They deal with stories too long to be handled in a column and they demonstrated his interest in and love for all those categories we listed above.

Barney was an excellent photographer. In fact he was a pioneer in photograph journalism, and his *Albums* contain unforgettable views of the region.

The Adirondacks, perhaps, were his first love and this region never had a better friend. Although he never lived here, he knew every dirt road, every waterfall, every winding stream. He hiked our trails, and swapped lies with other anglers at a multitude of fishing holes.

Barney lived a newspaperman's life. He was never very far from the smell of printer's ink. His first job at the age of ten was with the press and he served several capitol district newspapers in many capacities before he got his final assignment as columnist with the Adirondacks as his special beat.

He stood for all the right things. He opposed what we all know or should know is wrong. We who knew him as a colleague will miss him, and the State of New York and the Adirondacks have suffered a grievous loss.

December 10, 1986

Foreword

No one has ever offered a satisfactory explanation of why any one writes about anything, let alone about nature. Indeed, although there are some passages descriptive of nature in the Bible, and Virgil in his *Georgics* wrote eloquently of landscapes and the Reverend Gilbert White spent a lifetime putting on paper what he observed of nature in his Selborne parish in England, nature wasn't accepted as a proper subject for writers until the 19th century.

In America, Emerson composed his famous *Essay on Nature* which, however, was light on observation and heavy on the theme that nature made him feel good. This probably encouraged Thoreau to give us *Walden Pond* and *Cape Cod* which have inspired several generations of nature writers.

In England the Romantic poets were making writing about nature fairly respectable and turned the English-speaking world's attention to the satisfactions of observing nature. They, especially Wordsworth, made it, however, a mystique if not a religion and occasionally went overboard.

Matthew Arnold, their contemporary, admired Wordsworth's poems, but suggested that in one instance he had let sentiment overcome common sense. That was when Wordsworth said "To me the meanest flower that blows can give / Thoughts that lie too deep for tears."

A more serious error Wordsworth committed, in my opinion, was in this line in *Tintern Abbey*: "Knowing that nature never did betray the heart that loved her."

To that one might retort: tell that to the millions killed in earthquakes, tidal waves, volcanic eruptions, snow avalanches and mudslides, forest fires and floods. Nature is neutral, not a purposeful do-gooder, and can be both a benefactor and scourge of mankind.

What we have today on this planet is what Stephen Jay Gould would call a contingency of history. He represents the scientist as a nature writer and provides the reader with that additional something he wants above and beyond the Emersonian "feel good" and the purple adjectives of Wordsworth.

The fact is that nature writers have had a difficult time through the ages in justifying their preoccupation. Virgil was criticized for not devoting more of *Georgics* to the problems of agriculture. In his journals, Emerson paused to consider whether a grown man, at his age, should be spending time on such frivolous matters. The issue, it seems, has been posing the pleasures of nature writing against the demands of the practical utilitarian life.

As for me, I spent most of my 65 years as a newspaperman writing about politics, economics, wars, and possible solutions to human problems. I turned to nature writing for recreation, for fun.

But now, in a book entitled *End of Nature,* Bill McKibben of Johnsburg argues persuasively that nature is a subject not separate from politics but identical with the human problems for which we hold government and law accountable. During the two hundred plus years since James Watt invented the steam engine, our use of fossil fuels has so increased the amount of carbon dioxide in our atmosphere that the greenhouse effect threatens our planet with global warming. Doing nothing about this environmental disaster McKibben says, "will lead us, if not straight to hell, then straight to a place with a comparable temperature."

There are, he suggests, things we can do. Perhaps we should let God run this universe instead of ourselves playing at gods. We can preserve more of our nation and our planet as wilderness by planting more trees, preserving more open space. We can practice self restraint by limiting excessive population growth. We should concede that mankind is not the center of the universe but merely one part of a vast creation with duties and obligations as well as privileges. McKibben suggests that our salvation lies in something like the humility of Job. Whether or not we can achieve that is anybody's guess.

If we fail, my short essays on the changing seasons in the Adirondacks will be an irrelevance few will want to read.

SPRING

...Fair daffodils, we weep to see you haste away so soon

Robert Herrick

Early Spring

The marvels of nature which never cease to amaze us members of the human race are especially impressive at this time of year, that is, in early spring.

This is the season for synchronization. It is as if nature, like the Air Force commander who orders his group to "synchronize your watches," is instructing her plants and animals: "Okay, you guys, now synchronize your seasons, down to weeks, days, even hours."

Thus the robins arrive when ground temperature has risen to a thawing 32 degrees, making worms accessible. The swallows returning to Essex County, just as they do to Capistrano, arrive as the flying insects flutter in the wind for those birds which so expertly feed on the wing.

The day lilies which began putting out their saber-like leaves a month ago are holding back on the long stems for the blooms until all danger of frost has passed. A close inspection of the clumps of day lilies will fail even now to detect a single flower stem. But let the season progress even a few days and they will appear as from nowhere, budding, ready to break into glorious blooms at the proper time.

The millions of monarch butterflies may have already left their wintering grounds in that 20 acres of Mexico where they spend the cold months. But they will not arrive in our fields until the milkweed has emerged from the ground and leafed out for some 12 to 18 inches. As everyone knows, the milkweed is the essential food of the monarch larvae. The female lays her eggs on the young, sprouting milkweed so that the caterpillars will have tender leaves on which to feed. Watch the fields for young milkweed and you will be able to predict when the monarchs will again be with us.

The birds will not be interested in the return of the monarch. Because they subsist on a milkweed diet, they have an offensive taste and birds have long ago learned to avoid them. Another species of butterfly, however, learned long ago that its resemblance to the monarch allowed it to escape the attention of predatory birds. For that reason, the viceroy butterflies usually arrive simultaneously with the monarch.

The tent caterpillar is also capable of a smart job of synchronizing. The mother moth, in the fall, picks the early flowering fruit trees to lay her eggs. The tent with its crawling larvae is ready when the leaves appear. This is the time for home gardeners and orchardists to do their own synchronizing. Do it with a torch. A spray which kills the caterpillars may end in killing the birds.

Of course, we have a lot of synchronizing to do. As spring progresses, humans will be seen fishing in our fast-running brooks and rivers, or playing softball on the fresh carpet of grass. After all, synchronizing is merely being timely.

The Black Fly and the Dandelion

Last week the dandelions and the black flies appeared in Essex County, one a blessing, the other a curse. Trying to figure out how long this coincidental appearance has been going on, I find that winged insects first appeared 330 million years ago and flowers a mere 235 million years ago which suggests that this planet suffered a hundred million years of the bloodsucking insects before the arrival of the flower's beauty to compensate for that suffering.

You may say this is irrelevant, inasmuch as human-like creatures did not inhabit the earth until the Pleistocene age, some 750,000 years ago. It is relevant, however, to point out that when early humanoids arrived, they were greeted by something like the black fly and the dandelion. Meanwhile, the black flies were feasting on birds.

Presumably the black fly or its ancestors pursued the same life cycle it does today, laying eggs on sticks and stones in fast-running water, with the larvae and pupae continuing there until the newly hatched fly surfaces in a bubble of air, thence to fly away as a predator against man, beast, and fowl.

I can find no precise measure of the size of the black fly, but a reasonable estimate is that it would take twenty, lying end to end, to make an inch. There are 300 varieties worldwide and about thirty in North America. In our West, they are also known as the buffalo gnat, probably because like the buffalo, they are hump-backed. Some African species carry diseases dangerous to humans; in China there have been fatalities. In our country, they are mainly a nuisance to those who work or play outdoors, although for some people, with an allergic reaction to the poison they eject, they can have a delayed painful effect. Pipe-smokers are largely immune with a protection denied users of smokeless tobacco or cigarettes.

Our local variety attacks non-smoking humans as well as birds, chickens, some barnyard animals and especially ducklings. In Mississippi, there is a record of horses being smothered to death by black flies gathering in their nostrils. In Maine, a study by the U.S. Department of Agriculture showed black ducklings killed by a form of malaria carried by the black fly. A 1952 statement by the department suggested that the study of the relationship between insects and wildlife diseases had hardly begun, but should be promoted.

At that time, the department discussed using DDT against the black fly, but cautioned that dumping the chemical into the water could also kill fish. Since then, thanks largely to Rachel Carson, DDT has been outlawed. While some towns are using spraying from the air to control black flies, many environmentalists argue that all such chemicals are harmful and urge an end to it. As a pipe smoker, who can co-exist with black flies, I should be neutral. However, I vote against spraying.

As for the dandelion, its bright yellow flower heads dot our lawns and even creep up between the bricks of our walkways. Theirs is a brief life, followed by air-borne seeds and fluff that are disliked by many homeowners who go to the expense of buying lawn fertilizer mixed with a chemical to kill broad-leafed weeds. I'm against that because it also kills clover. Besides, dandelions are easier to live with than the black fly. Our lives consist of an eternal compromise with nature, a kind of deal we have negotiated throughout our years on this planet. We glory in the beauty and abundance. But we concede we may pay a modest price.

The Season's First Butterfly

It was April 29 when I saw my first cabbage white butterfly of the season. True to form, he (or she) did not appear singly, but with a mate, and the two, although they had developed from pupae only minutes before, were already engaged in the ritual of mating.

The March-April 1975 issue of *The Conservationist* contained an unforgettable article by the Cornell entomologist, Arthur Shapiro, entitled, "Why the Cabbage White Butterfly Zigs and Zags."

"Today we know what the cabbage white is up to," Professor Shapiro wrote. "That zig-zag flight is really a very effective way for a small airborne animal to look for something. What it's looking for is a matter of sex."

If it's male, he is looking for a receptive female. If it's female, she's looking for a cabbage plant on which to lay her egg, he said.

But on April 29, my cabbage plants had not even been planted. Professor Shapiro explained that besides the cultivated garden vegetable, the cabbage has many members, some of them wild and already growing in the early spring.

The cabbage butterfly can do nicely on wild mustard, either the winter or summer variety, on yellow rocket, peppergrass, watercress, crinkleroot, horseradish and turnip.

All belong to the family *Cruciferae* or cross-bearers, and have a peppery taste derived from mustard oil glycosydes, a compound common to members of the family.

The female will lay her eggs only in plants containing this compound because the larvae which will hatch from her eggs eat only the leaves so flavored. The cabbage white caterpillars are fortunate in that almost all other insects find this compound poisonous.

The female lays one egg at a time which will hatch in about a week into a caterpillar. It will eat voraciously for two or three weeks, then stop eating and enter the pupal stage. In ten days, the pupa becomes a butterfly. In the North, there are three broods a season. In the South, as many as six.

The peculiar sex life of the cabbage butterfly has been noticed by poets as well as entomologists. Robert Graves wrote:

> *The butterfly, a cabbage white,*
> *(His honest idiocy of flight)*
> *Will never know, it is too late*
> *To master the art of flying straight.*
> *He lurches here and there by guess*
> *By God and hope and hopelessness.*

An Early Bird - The Phoebe

There's an old adage that the early bird catches the worm. For us, perhaps the earliest is the phoebe, but he arives from the South even before the worms surface or the flying insects (which the phoebe prefers) fly.

The phoebe will appear as early as mid March, and perched upright on a leafless limb, his tail bobbing both horizontally and vertically, may even dart out and catch a snowflake in his beak. For practice probably.

Eating in flight is a characteristic of the phoebe which would classify him with the large flycatchers like the kingbird, the middle-sized ones like the peewee and the olive-sided flycatcher, or the miniatures like the least flycatcher and the alder flycatcher.

But the taxonomists who attached the Latin names to birds place the phoebe as a *sayornis*, the kingbird as a *tyrannus*, and the little flycatchers as *empidonax*. To me, most of the members of these families have not only common habits but are physically similar, differing mainly in size.

Like the phoebe, they tend to be dull gray-brown in color with a high, almost pointed skull like a crest.

My introduction to the phoebe came thirty years ago watching Dick Lawrence boiling sap in his sugarhouse. The phoebe perched on a beam, near what I took to be his last year's nest. It was made of moss and mud. The bird paid no attention to us but repeatedly announced its name.

I have read that the phoebe never nests in trees but prefers a location under a roof, like the sugarhouse, a barn, a carport or garage, a woodshed, or even your front porch. But the phoebe likes to be near water, and you'll often find the phoebe nests under a bridge or culvert over a rushing stream.

It is the female who is the nest builder and she sometimes works on a second nest while the male watches over and feeds the young. A second nest is often needed because, for some reason, the phoebe nests are plagued with red mites which in extreme instances will kill the nestlings.

While mud and moss are the favorite construction materials, horse hairs, sheep's wool and chicken feathers are utilized when available.

John Bull, New York State's most authoritative ornithologist, says the phoebe is double brooded, with an average of four eggs to the nest. Egg dates are April 20 to August 4; nestlings May 13 to August 10; fledglings June 9 to August 24.

If the white-throat sparrow was the favorite bird of John Burroughs, the phoebe was a close second in his affections. Oddly, he always spoke of him as the phoebe bird.

They are brave little creatures, ignoring people and people-traffic, and they have been known to chase away crows and smaller hawks from their nesting area.

Phoebus in Greek means radiant, which the phoebe bird is not, and in Greek mythology, it is applied to Phoebus Apollo, the radiant sun god. But it also stands for Artemis, or Diana, the goddess of the hunt. When the phoebe bird evolved its song, from which it got its name, it certainly didn't have the pantheon of Greek gods in mind.

The Water Strider

It was the first really warm day of April, with the thermometer reading over 70 in the sun. The brook was running swiftly but was more calm in pools where large rocks had created something like a dam.

Looking down on one of these pools I witnessed for the first time in my life the birth of the water strider. These are the insects which stride on the surface of freshwater ponds and would go unnoticed except for the ripples they cause.

What I saw, I think, was the moment directly after hatching. On both sides of the pool the newly hatched striders were gathered in colonies, giving the surface of water a gelatinous look. As the individual striders broke away from the colony, they glided gracefully across the water, making sudden, swift forays against their prey, invisible to me but no doubt obvious to the microscopic eyes of the striders.

At maturity, the strider is about five millimeters long. To grasp the significance of this figure, know that it takes two and half centimeters to make an inch, and ten millimeters to make a centimeter.

It has six legs, four of which are twice the length of its body, and the two short ones at its head are no doubt used mainly to capture its prey. The four long jointed legs keep the body out of the water while the strider skips over the surface.

On the morning I watched them, the sun shone and was reflected in two or three drops of what I presumed to be water on the body or legs, but might have been some material carried over from the egg. It was as if each strider carried a set of headlamps that made it more visible from above but still unseen by the tiny insects below on which the strider feeds.

The water strider belongs to the suborder *Gymnocerata* and the family *Gerridae*. The Peterson guide to insects says some striders have wings. If so, they failed to exhibit them that morning.

For me it was like witnessing a miracle but of course much more meaningful for the striders. Since the autumn they had existed as eggs, microscopic bits of protein, locked beneath the ice of the brook, awaiting that warm day in spring when the temperature would instruct them to hatch. Thus they began the brief life which would end soon after mating and the laying of eggs from which a new generation of striders would emerge.

If there is a limnologist among my readers who can correct the errors of a lay observer, please speak up. Science progressed by refining, confirming or rejecting the presumptious guesses of us amateurs.

The Adirondack Guide

Sharpie Swan has been doing research for the Adirondack Center Museum into the history of this region, its customs, the means by which the people got their livelihood, and individuals who stand out in the journals of their contemporaries.

The Adirondack guides are probably the most memorable of such individuals.

Mr. Swan suggests that the skills which enabled the first settlers in these mountains to survive were those that made the Adirondack guide such a valuable companion to the city visitors and sportsmen who came later. The guides knew the territory. They were familiar with the habits of the deer, the black bear and bobcat. They could point to the cove on the lake or a bend in the brook where the most fish could be found. And they were woodsmen who could erect a leanto or build a light-weight boat as needed.

Most of them had a touch of showmanship and enjoyed center stage around the campfire where they told incredible yarns of hunting, fishing and deadly winter storms. Mr. Swan says they earned $2 to $3 a day for their services, a handsome salary for the time.

The late Pieter Fosburgh once wrote an essay in which he said the proper pronounciation of their vocation was "goid."

One of the most colorful was Orson Scofield Phelps (1817-1905), known as "Old Mountain." Much quoted was his comment that standing up on Mount Marcy gave him the feeling of "heaven uphistedness." Operating mainly in Keene Valley, he identified with his "mountings" and guided mountain climbers as well as hunters and fishermen. His contemporaries described him as having matted hair, a reddish beard and an aversion to soap and water. "Soap is something I ain't got no kind of use for, " he said. "I don't believe in this eternal sozzling."

John Cheney (1800-1887) was known as the "Mighty Hunter." Local records say that in his first thirteen years operating near the iron works at Tahawus, with his birch-handled 11-inch pistol, he killed 600 deer, 400 sable, 19 moose, 48 bears, 7 wildcats, 6 wolves, 30 otters and one panther. He is said to have guided the first ascent of Mount Marcy in 1837. He is also credited with a memorable quote: "It makes me feel what it is to have all creation placed under one's feet. There are woods there which it would take a lifetime to hunt. Mountains that seem shouldering each other up and away, heaven knows where."

There were others, including Mitchell Sabattis and the Moody Brothers.

Mr. Swan says that after 1870 the role of the guide as hunter and trapper began to decline, a consequence of the increasing pressures of population and encroaching civilization. Some continued to earn a living "doing the lakes," that is, paddling city visitors at the hotels around the ponds.

So passed a remarkable breed of men, wilderness-wise, intelligent, competent and many of them with a touch of poetry in their love of these mountains.

The Great Blue Heron

Whenever you see a great blue heron flying over or wading and feeding on the lake shore, you cannot help but get excited. You rush to tell others. The heron is a magnificent bird. It stands, as adult, about four feet high. In flight, it tucks its long neck in like the figure *s*, with its long legs straight out behind.

According to the experts there have always been a lot of herons in the Adirondacks, but they seemed scarce, according to W. E. Benning, because the area "contains a vast amount of remote sections... Lack of coverage by observers may account for at least a part of this seeming scarcity in this part of the state."

Although the great blue heron nests most frequently in wooded swamps, its nests will also be found in upland forests at some distance from water. John Bull cites "as many as 11 nests in a single large elm."

If there is a single pattern in the habits of the great blue heron, it has not been yet discovered. Bull describes it as "both sedentary and migratory." The Peterson guide map has it breeding from southern Canada to the Gulf states, and while mainly wintering in the South, some great blue herons stay north year-round.

Prof. Charles Mitchell of the State University of New York at Plattsburgh believes there's a lot more we ought to know about the blue heron and is heading a project to study the birds's habits, especially on Valcour Island.

Last summer he counted 432 heron nests on the island, which he says establishes Valcour as one of the largest and most significant heronry in New York State. "Despite these facts," Prof. Mitchell says, "little is known about the herons."

The Return of the Brown-Headed Cowbirds

The brown-headed cowbirds are back. Known scientifically as *Molothrus ater*, they travel in flocks, slightly smaller than the red-winged black birds. It is the male that has the brown head but the female has the reputation.

That reputation is for promiscuity, compared with most other birds which are monogamous for life. Although we are warned against applying our standards, moral or otherwise, to members of the animal kingdom, we cannot resist this exercise in anthropomorphism.

We humans who are accused of undergoing an era of permissiveness, nevertheless are shocked, when we think about it, of the immorality of the cowbirds. The female mates when she feels like it, with any male brown-head that comes along. She has, in fact, a stable of studs.

Her odium, from the human point of view, has another facet. The female cowbird lays her eggs in the nest of song birds and since, when hatched, her nestling is larger than the legitimate occupant, there are known instances wherein the little song bird is pushed from the nest while the mother songbird spends her efforts feeding the oversized young tresspasser.

She makes a noise which can hardly be called a song. It resembles nothing more than a human upchucking.

Perhaps the female cowbirds serve a purpose, after all, in projecting an image of what we ought to abhor.

It speaks for the prodigality of nature that the season that brings us the cowbird also gladdens our gardens and hillsides with what the poet Wordsworth called the "host of golden daffodils." Their value derives in part from their early appearance which Shakespeare noted "comes before the swallow dares."

It is a member of the *Narcissus* genus along with the jonquil and the book says that it is ubiquitous in eastern United States and northern Europe ("But not in Scotland," it adds). Originally, a wildflower in the Old World, it has been cultivated in our land and blooms in forty color variations, almost the entire spectrum except for blue. But most of us are willing to settle for the brilliant yellow, announcing that spring is well on the way even if the thermometer seems stuck in the lower forties.

One autumn planting will reward the gardener for three or four years but the book says you should replant after that.

The *Narcissus* is the genus; the family is *Amaryllidaceae*, and is a native to central Europe and the Mediterranean. The genus is named for the handsome young Greek God, son of the river God Cephissus and the nymph Leiroppe. The story goes that he was warned that he would have a long life unless he looked at his own features. He could not resist the temptation, like a lot of our handsome and vain young people, and he pined away and died beside the pool where he saw his image. The flower that bears his name is said to have grown on the spot where he died.

We humans cannot create the flower but we sure can make up a pretty story. As for the daffodil's brief visit, we say with the poet Herrick: "We weep to see thee haste away so soon."

Daffodil Time

> *"I saw a crowd*
> *A host of golden daffodils."*

William Wordsworth's poem celebrates the glory of early spring when the daffodils, or jonquils, or narcissuses, whichever word you prefer for that flower, suddenly are in bloom. But there is an earlier poem by Robert Herrick which illustrates how quickly the early season changes:

> *"Fair daffodils, we weep to see*
> *You haste away so soon."*

That is the joy and sorrow of early spring which is a matter of moment, or seems to be.

One moment there are buds. Almost as you watch the buds are leaves, or flowers.

A walk around one's garden at this season reminds one that all trees have flowers, some so tiny you never see them, some like the shag-bark hickory, very showy. The flowers of the pines are the candles which exude pollen; the flowers of the birch are the catkins which come before the leaves.

I'm reminded of a drawing which caught a woods scene just as the snow retreated and nature's obvious alchemy had barely begun. In the foreground is a double tamarack tree, our only deciduous evergreen. Only a few days after the artist finished the work, their lithe limbs were dotted with green buds which began the quick march to needles and toward the small cones characteristic of that species, still to come.

The leaves of the sugar maple are like the wings of a butterfly emerging from the cocoon, soft, damp and wrinkled. But again, in another moment, they will open and become firm.

All of us await with impatience the burst of electric rose and purple in the flowering crab trees, and days later the lilac blooms.

But impatience is wasted. The thing is to seize the moment and see what there is to see before the moment passes.

If there is time for reflection it should be on how nature rewards foresight and planning. The tulips and daffodils are here because someone, looking ahead to these spring days, in the chill of last fall on their hands and knees planted the bulbs which now confound us with their brilliance and beauty.

Backpacking in May
Blue Mountain Lake, New York

We are of an age that prizes its comforts and travelers, especially, set great store by them. They travel by jet plane, perhaps, and their gravest complaint is the two-drink limit. Or they travel by automobile over fast, four-lane highways with a motel unit with wall-to-wall carpets awaiting them, and if the television doesn't work, the inn-keeper will send around another set.

The air traveler sees one piece of reality and the automobile traveler another. And both pieces are eminently satisfying to the more commonly felt needs of the credit-card carrying members of the traveling public. But there is another large chunk of reality accessible only to those prepared for the rigors and discomforts of foot travel.

Some of its virtues are obvious. For him who rides shank's mare, the course is not set in advance by the blueprints of the highway engineers nor the navigational maps of the airline pilots. The foot traveler's options as to course are almost limitless. Speed of travel is his own decision and the extent of his journey determined only by the time at his disposal and the durability of his arches. My family had unanimously agreed that our travels this summer would be largely by foot. Of course, we would cover the greater distances by car, from our home to the edge of a wilderness from which we should start our interior journey. Selecting the general area was easy. In Hamilton County, the largest county in the Adirondacks, two-thirds of its land or 740,000 acres are within the forest preserve, studded with lakes and ponds and laced with running streams. There remained only the task of the scout as an advance party of one who would pinpoint the course of the family expedition and report back on necessary equipment.

I accepted the assignment and to carry it out chose the trail to Cascade Pond. It starts at the forest ranger's cottage on U.S. 28 just south of the village of Blue Mountain Lake. Don Perryman, the ranger, a pleasant, red-haired young man, told me there was a leanto overlooking the pond, just three and a half miles along the trail. "There's probably some fire wood under the shelter," he said, which was comforting because a steady rain was falling.

"It's three o'clock now," said Don, "so you'll have four hours of daylight to get there and get settled."

He walked with me a couple of hundred yards to where the trail markers began. On my own, then, I slogged along, skirting the state campsite on Lake Durant and pushing step by step deeper into the wilderness.

It was early May, before the underbrush had leafed, and one could see a hundred yards into the forest on either side of the trail. Although this was part of the Adirondack forest preserve which, under the constitution, must be kept "forever wild," it was not virgin forest. It was bought by the state from lumber companies a decade or two ago, after the merchantable timber had been logged off. Thus only a few very old and very large trees, mostly beech, remained. The greater number were second or third growth.

The floor of the forest was brown and yellow with the leaves of last autumn. Only at the edge of the trail, a former logging road at this point, where the sunlight had filtered through, was there the green of spring vegetation. Here and there among the green were white trillium and pale blue hepatica.

On the trail itself, the leaves underfoot had turned black, the same color of the highly acid soil enriched by hundreds of years of rotting vegetation. The rain was now turning this nice black soil into muck and the walking became more arduous. Often it was necessary to leave the trail to skirt a fallen tree, blown down by a recent wind, but it was easy to find one's way again, thanks to the numerous blue trail markers nailed to the trees by the Conservation Department trail crews.

Now and then a chipmunk literally high-tailed it across the trail and safely from a nearby branch peered at me curiously. Over the sound of the rain I could hear woodpeckers hammering away high in some dead trees. But for some reason the woods were otherwise strangely quiet.

After an hour's walk the pack bore more heavily on my back and my sleeping bag, tied in a tight roll and hung over my shoulder, was soggy. I had foolishly come off without a hat or a cap and the rain poured down my face and into my eyes. I recalled the Admiral Crichton's stern lecture to his former employer who had neglected to salvage a hairpin which he saw on the beach of their desert island. Neither a hiker in the wilderness nor a castaway can afford mistakes. I made a headband of my handkerchief which protected my eyes until it too, was soaked.

I found myself acting throughout with care and deliberation. A false step and a sprained ankle could prove a disaster. A slip of the jack-knife blade on my hand could leave me helpless. He travels fastest who travels alone, perhaps, but he who travels alone by foot in the wilderness must prefer safety to speed.

After an hour and a half I came to the registration board which the Conservation Department had erected where the trail forked. To the left was Stephen's Pond, a half mile; to the right Cascade Pond, a mile. I wrote my name in the book, the date, and my destination and watched the ink blur in the rain.

It was after five when I heard the sound of the waterfall which announced I was close to my destination. On a precarious log, swaying with the weight of my pack, I crossed the cascade and reached the shelter of the leanto.

It was a relief to shed my burden but depressing to discover that despite my raincoat I was wet through and through. I sat under the eaves of the shelter and looked out at the lake, not exactly at peace with the world but not wholly unhappy. The long, high Blue Ridge Mountain was blanketed in mist and the water of the pond danced forlornly in the slanting rain. An Adirondack lake (or pond, for the words are almost interchangeable) had a right to its moods, I decided, and one must take the dour with the bright.

My immediate problem was a fire, and it was obvious that even Daniel Boone could not have kindled one in the open fireplace in that heavy rain. Fortunately some hunters had left an old covered stove in the clearing. The few sticks of wood in the leanto were dry but were too large to use to start a fire. However with the curly fingers of birch bark, paper thin and flammable despite their wetness, I managed to kindle a feeble blaze. It did not bring my water to a boil but warmed it enough for a potable cup of instant coffee which I drank with a cold sandwich from my knapsack.

At eight I crawled into my damp sleeping bag and dozed fitfully with rain drumming on the roof of the leanto. It was the sudden absence of that sound, when the rain stopped, that woke me. I saw streaks of blue in the sky and then the clouds parted and a full moon shown. My watch was exactly at nine. I built up the fire which was now hot enough to accept even wet wood and hanging my outer garments over the old stove with a stick succeeded in drying them out. The stars were appearing one by one as the clouds scudded away and it seemed that the beauty of the pond by moonlight compensated for the damp and chill of the night.

When I returned at last to my sleeping bag (which was still wet) I slept more soundly, only to be awakened at two by the sound of another downpour. I had another cup of lukewarm coffee, a comforting pipe, and some wakeful hours for meditation. The hot top of the old stove hissed and spat as each drop of rain hit it, and with that pleasant sound in my ear I slept again.

The clouds were thick and heavy when daylight descended but the rain had stopped. The woods were now alive with sound. The call of the white-throated sparrow seemed to come from all sides. Jays were crying and sparrows chip-chipping, and there were other songs I could not identify. A pair of myrtle warblers, all black and white and yellow, flitted about in a little spruce.

As I stood gazing off at the mountain across the pond a snuffling noise at my feet caused me to look down, and there was an enormous porcupine. I shouted at him as if he were a vagrant dog and, startled, he turned and ambled down the slope to the pond, carefully scrutinized the base of a hemlock, decided against climbing it, and moved out of sight. A few minutes later I could see him advance with great dignity and sure of foot across the log that spanned the waterfall and disappear into the woods.

With my dry wood exhausted and every uncovered stick soaked beyond use, I gave up the idea of a hot breakfast. Packed up I started again for civilization. Soon the sun came out and a chorus of bird songs followed me. In the soft black mud there were deer tracks and the squirrels and chipmunks were everywhere. I recalled that a biologist in the Conservation Department had predicted an enormous increase in the rodent population due to the heavy crop of beech nuts last autumn.

The ruts and declivities in the trail were filled with water and in several of them I saw little red salamanders swimming about.

During my wakeful night I had already weighed the price I had paid in discomfort for the satisfaction of my journey. I had concluded that the price was not too high. I had come close in this Adirondack wilderness to the reality that Henry Thoreau found in the Maine woods and that Henry Beston had grasped that winter on Cape Cod.

With the sun at my back, drying out my soggy coat collar, and my boots keeping time to the drummings of the woodpeckers, I knew I was right. Besides, since the average rainfall in the Adirondacks is four inches a month, that's one inch a week or only one seventh of an inch a day, which leaves room for a lot of sunshine. But next time I'll remember to wear a hat.

Copyright © 1968 by N.Y. Times
reprinted by permission

The Miracle of Mutation

The new-born child does not come into this world knowing how to read, or how to apply the theorem of Pythagoras to a geometry problem. These are skills that have to be learned because, science tells us, acquired characteristics cannot be inherited. But the baby is equipped with a number of essential pieces of knowledge and instincts: how to suckle, how to cry when hungry or uncomfortable, and the fear of falling. These, science tells us, are indeed inherited through millions of years of evolution. They are in our genes, and all living matter in the plant and animal kingdoms has genes.

But how does that change come about, Darwin asked, and the answer was in that miracle, mutation.

Mutation must indeed be miraculous, if it can change an ape into something more human-like, and a snake into a bird. Of course, this took a very long time because such changes were gradual. But not always gradual. Professor Stephen Jay Gould suggests that what has been thought gradual was also explosive and sudden. Like the Cambrian period, 500 million years ago when trolobites became fish, and soft shelled creatures became hard shelled; and 300 million years later when the dinosaurs roamed the earth, only to disappear mysteriously to leave a vacancy filled by creatures that eventually became us.

The important thing to know about mutations is that all of them are not helpful. Only those which give the mutatee an advantage over other forms of life survive. The four-leaf clover is a mutation which provides little if any advantage; therefore, the three-leaf clover continues to dominate our lawns. The babies born with flippers instead of arms to mothers who took the drug thalidomide were a mutation which did not survive because the flippers were a disadvantage in a world of two-armed, two-handed individuals.

One may argue that this was not a mutation because it was caused by a drug. But we know very little about what causes mutations. Presumably, they are accidents, but accidents which are caused by an external happening, like radiation. There is some evidence that some historic mutations followed the fall of thousands of meteors, with whatever radiation they exuded. In view of the fact that radiation from nuclear plants is a constant danger to this civilization, we may be in for some shocking mutations in coming years.

Society is not hospitable to tinkering with genes, certainly not our own, but even those of plants and animals, for fear of creating monsters. Just the other day a scientist who was experimenting with the genes of the elm tree without the proper license, in an effort to make them immune to Dutch elm blight, was reprimanded.

The social insects, that is, those that live in colonies like bees, ants, wasps, etc., have a gene for what Professor E. O. Wilson calls altruism, which he says accounts for their ability to subordinate selfish, individual appetites to the common good. The professor suggested at one time that *Homo sapiens* contained a similar gene, but that was an unpopular theory and he was compelled to retract it. A mutation that would provide humans with such a gene, universally distributed, and in such numbers as to change mankind's character, would be, perhaps, the fulfillment of the Biblical prophecy of a Kingdom of God on Earth.

Such a development doesn't seem to be in the cards for the near future. In fact, humans with an overdose of that altruism gene do not fare well. Jesus of Nazareth, who had more of it than anyone else we know about, was killed by the leaders of the society in which he demonstrated that genetic quality.

But we live in hope and the mutation is the key to that hope. Until that happens to the human race, we must work on the acquired characteristics, the things that are not inherited, but must be learned by every new generation. That suggests that we must teach our children not only the old verities, but whatever is new and useful and healthy for this race.

I guess that means more money for education, right?

Seasons

Professor Leighly of Berkeley who wrote the section on seasons for the *Encyclopedia Britannica* says that actually there are only two seasons, summer and winter, that spring and autumn are merely transitional periods, "hardly worthy of names coordinate in rank with those of summer and winter." We have names for spring and autumn, he says, only because of the yearly round of chores performed by the European husbandman, including the Roman from whose word for sowing, *satio*, the word season is derived.

This is academic pedantry at its worst. It ignores the fact that all of nature is change and transition, with past and future locked into the present, a becoming and a going, a borning and a dying. The white snow that mantles our countryside in February is a shroud for the season that is passing; it is also the swaddling clothes for the new season about to be born.

Language means nothing if it does not express the reality of humankind's experience, and what in our experience is more relevant than the chores of the husbandman who provided our sustenance ever since human society advanced from hunting to agriculture?

All of which suggests that Henry David Thoreau was in the right place on a rainy April 19, 1852 when he chose a barn on Baker's farm to watch the coming of spring. "Sat in the dry meadow-hay, where the mice nest" he wrote. "To sit there, rustling the hay, just beyond the reach of the rain while the storm roars without."

I have my favorite barn, a refuge in a spring rain and a vantage point to observe the small changes, day by day, and hour by hour which herald the coming of spring. The rain may turn to snow, as often happens in March, sending me back to my fireside, and my neighbors, busy tapping the maples in their sugarbush, back to their kitchens. But given a warm day there will be much to see and hear.

The red-winged blackbirds are back by mid-March, and under the eaves of the barn, a phoebe bird is building a nest. In my view the trees are still leafless, and the calls I hear come from jays and crows with now and then the mating call of a chickadee, a call that is similar yet different from the song of the white-throat which will affirm the arrival of spring more certainly than the March 20th equinox.

Actually the day when we have twelve hours of sun and twelve of night comes about three days earlier here. I suspect the longer hours of solar warmth affect the body chemistry of humans as it does that of the rest of nature's creatures. In the sixty-one days from March 1 to April 30, the amount of sun increases from eleven hours and seventeen minutes to thirteen hours and fifty-seven minutes, a total of two hours and forty minutes, almost three minutes a day.

This will melt the snow that from my barn door I can see in patches under the trees, and on protected slopes of the meadow. But the thaw is not an unmixed blessing. My yard becomes a sea of mud which makes us grateful for the bootscraper screwed to the back porch.

Back in the woods, on the dirt roads used by logging trucks, the two to three feet of frost in the earth become that much mud, which stops logging activity for more than a month.

By then, of course, April is here and for the countryman there can be no finer time. The ice is gone from the ponds. The skunk cabbage and the hepatica which earlier pushed through the snow have been joined alongside the roadsides by the trillium. The willow trees herald the season with bright yellow leaves, almost chartreuse. The maples, birches and poplars are putting forth their flowers, giving a new tinge of color to the forest. The peepers are noisy. The fishermen are moving in for the first days of the trout season. The robins are on every lawn and are far along with their nest building and mating.

Still there are April showers to commend me again to my observation post just inside the barn, while Professor Leighly's "husbandmen" are turning the black earth into long, straight furrows with their tractor-drawn plows, scattering manure, and preparing to seed the land for another harvest.

Frost is still a possibility; in fact the U.S. Department of Agriculture dates our last killing frost, on an average, at May 15. But until October, we have an average of 150 growing days, enough time for the family to plant, nurture and reap garden vegetables.

Since there is a bit of the husbandman in all of us, on the issue of spring, the Professor can go his way and we go ours, inspired, reverent and thankful for that uncomparable season.

Meet the Hawthorn

In our rather chilly zone, dogwood does not flourish, and for a white-flowered tree in the spring we have come to depend almost exclusively on the shadblow or service berry. But the shadblow flowers only briefly and the blossoms are gone, as their name suggest, after the shad run in the Hudson River is completed. Apple blossoms may continue to deck the landscape for another few days, but if one wants more white to relieve the green of our roadsides, it will have to be something else.

That something else, according to Mrs. Cynthia Dunn of Wadhams, is the hawthorn. Her suggestion sent me to my trees and shrubs books, and to a more observant walk in my own woods.

The books tell us that the hawthorn of the genus *Crataegus* is represented in at least 100 species in North America with some botanists putting the figure closer to a thousand. It was long used as a boundary for fields in England where it made a stout, thorny hedge impassable by horses and cattle.

It may be identified by its alternate, simple leaves, and its clusters of white or pink flowers, followed by showy red, blue or black fruit, known as haws. But of course the ultimate evidence is its thorns, which are obvious, very sharp, and efficient.

The hawthorn tree is medium sized, averaging fifteen to twenty-five feet. I found it in the wild growing under pine trees, surviving but not what might be called really prospering. Many of the trees seemed to creep literally along the grounds, rather than fight with other vegetation for a place in the sun. It is, it should be noted, very amenable to pruning.

Properly cared for, hawthorns can become attractive ornamental flowering trees in plantings around the house or near the flower garden. One of the finest collection of hawthorn in the world, according to the *Encyclopedia Britannica*, is found in the Genesee Valley Gardens in Rochester, New York. There is also a collection at the Arnold Arboretum of Harvard University at Jamaica Plains, Mass.

The encyclopedia warns that hawthorn flowers "emit the faint odour of decayed fish," but one may enjoy their bright beauty without insisting on close encounter. For the superstitious, a disadvantage may be the myth that to bring a hawthorn bough into the home portends death. Bees and butterflies avoid the bad smell of the blossoms; consequently pollination is carried on only by flies who find decayed fish to their taste.

In any case, the advantages of hawthorn far outweigh the disadvantages, and its existence in our woods attests to its suitability for cultivation locally. I write in the hope that this piece will encourage a wide planting of this otherwise pleasant ornamental shrub.

An Apology for Anthropods

At this season in the North Country when black flies and mosquitos are the scourge that discourages a hike on the mountain trail or even a family gathering on the lawn of a summer afternoon, a public opinion poll would register an almost unanimous conclusion that insects are an enemy to be exterminated. But like abortion, flag burning and the Adirondack Commission report, the insect is an issue on which there are at least two sides.

Back in May, *The New York Times* op-ed page carried an eloquent column by Anna Quindlen complaining of the plague of gypsy moth caterpillars and other bugs which soiled the potato salad on the picnic table, parachuted into her hair, and generally made life miserable. Her call to arms against insects provoked a passionate response from readers who condemned what they perceived as a demand for widespread spraying of toxic pesticides, and from at least one thoughtful entomologist who argued that "there must be more effective teaching about the positive role of insect life in classrooms, museums, outreach programs, and nature center workshops."

Perhaps the time is ripe, wrote Curator Allen M. Young of the Milwaukee Public Museum, for a "bug-rights lobby."

Like Ms. Quindlen, I have my grudge against certain insects. A black fly bite leaves me red, swollen, and itching for days. But I am happy that most of our Adirondack town governments have ended the spraying that killed birds, wildlife, and fish larvae, as well as insects. More importantly, I share Mr. Young's fascination for insects as a class, known as anthropods, and appreciate their role in making this planet habitable for us and the food chain on which we survive.

As for survival, no one does it better than these anthropods. There are 700,000 known species of them and during their 200 million years on earth they have undergone little change. Whatever the cataclysm that destroyed the dinosaurs, it was survived by the insects, and if a nuclear war or a global explosion should at sometime in the future again devastate the planet, we can be sure that some of these insects, having crawled under a rock, will come forth again, reinstitute the cycle of life, and give aid to another Mother Eve to perpetuate a human race.

The human is a social animal. The Adams and Eves learned early that they must work together as families, as tribes, as a society. But we have never brought social life to the perfection that some insects have, such as the honey bees and the ants.

Research has discovered how the bees communicate in their search for food, how they signal direction and distance. Insects have also developed a reproductive system for protecting their progeny from predators or bad weather. We know it as metamorphosis: the egg which hatches into a caterpillar, the caterpillar which spins a cocoon called a chrysalis, and the beautiful butterfly or the moth that emerges to continue the cycle of life. But what ingenuity! The monarch butterfly eats only milkweed which tastes so bad birds won't eat the butterfly. And another species of butterfly, the viceroy, mimics the colors of the monarch, which frightens the birds away even though it would taste just fine.

If this isn't enough to impress one with the genius of insects, consider the results of some research made public recently by Professor Philip J. DeVries of the University of Texas. Some caterpillars, he reported, make sounds to call crowds of ants to surround them to act as bodyguards protecting them against wasps. The sound, described as a musical thumping, is so faint it can be detected by the human ear only with the help of tiny microphones, but it is heard by ants and they respond, to fight off the wasps and save the endangered caterpillar.

The insects were here before us and by all odds will be here long after we have gone. It seems to make sense, in any case, for us to value their presence and learn as much about them as we can for whatever good it may do us.

SUMMER

*Man in his prime
Is man in a hurry.
One says he's busy as a bee.
He doesn't notice the summer solstice
But the bee does.*

Observing Nature

I don't know how it was in other places but in my hometown all the kids believed that thunder and lightning were caused by clouds bumping into each other. If you enjoy observing nature and put great value on it, you must be prepared for some mistakes. Our error lay in our failure to take observation far enough. Had we noticed that the mist which lay on the ground was, like the clouds, soft, we would not have concluded that the bumping of the clouds caused anything. Besides, as the wind blew all the clouds in one direction there was no bumping.

Observing nature, however, is a time-honored activity of young people. I remember my first visitation of the 17-year cicada which we called locusts. I was 9 years old and I'll never forget that squeaky, scratchy song they sang nor the lifeless shells they left behind.

Gilbert White, an Anglican priest, born in 1720, who lived out his life in the English parish of Selborne, spent that life mainly in observing nature around him. He wrote that "nature is so full that that district produces the most variety that is most examined." That was another way of saying that the more you look the more you can see.

Even if you are a botanist or an ornithologist, you are bound to come upon some surprising facts, but if you are a self-taught layman, as most of us are, the surprises are limitless.

Visiting Florida last March, I was surprised to count fifty (more or less) robins gathered along a telephone wire preparing to fly north. They flew off before morning and I wondered how far they traveled each day. The trick was not to arrive in Essex County, as I saw it, until the soil thawed and the worms were available.

The robins at our place were busily nest building during the last half of April. One pair had positioned the nest in the loops of a garden hose that hung on the wall of the woodshed. On May 5, the three eggs had hatched. The big surprise was that by May 17, they were fledglings and had escaped to the trees and lawn to earn their own livelihood.

At this moment the unanswered question is will the couple utilize the old nest for another brood or must it make another?

Note: The robins returned to that nest twice. The third brood consisted of four which left the nest August 1.

An Answer to the Chickadee Puzzle

The chickadee, as we know, gets its common name from its song, which almost literally mimics the word. But the chickadee has another song, described as its mating call, heard in the spring as the winter flocks break up, and the pairs retreat to their own territory to breed.

The mating call has a unique melody, which has been described as halfway between the flat two syllables of the phoebe and the long quavering song of the white-throat sparrow.

For some of us, the chickadee's mating call has been a puzzle. It is often heard in late winter and early fall, when the breeding season has not begun or when it has long passed. Is the chickadee over-sexed? Or are we merely ignorant of the call's significance?

I think I found the answer in a brilliant piece of research and study by Professor Susan M. Smith of Mt. Holyoke College in South Hadley, Mass., published in a recent issue of *Natural History*. Miss Smith began her study of chickadees in 1979, banding the individuals with differently colored labels visible from some distance, and watching them at the local bird feeders in the lawns and gardens of her neighbors.

When summer ends, and the clutch of five to nine eggs have hatched and fledglings are off on their own, the flocks re-form, usually consisting of five pair. But joining the flock will be several unpaired individuals which Miss Smith calls floaters.

The floaters may be male or female. They are tolerated but apparently not welcomed by the regulars, and they may switch from one flock to another, obviously looking for a mate, a nest and breeding territory.

There is a high mortality among chickadees, according to Miss Smith, and each year many fall victim to cats and the sharp-skinned hawk. And a certain number, of course, must die of old age or whatever diseases infect birds.

Floaters never pair with each other, but when a regular dies, a floater arrives promptly to take his or her place.

If one can imagine these lonely floaters living on the edge of an organized flock of happily married monogamous couples, it is easy to understand their eagerness to enter a flock with an established position. I would expect an impatience which begins even before winter has passed, and painful frustration if no mate has been found after summer has ended.

Thus I suggest, those early and late mating calls come from the unrequited floaters. It is their way of announcing to new widows and widowers that love, companionship and procreation are available.

Of course, Professor Smith may not agree with me but for the moment it must stand as a plausible answer to the puzzle.

Remembering Isaak Walton

All the figures for the Lake Champlain International Fishing Derby are not yet in, but judging from the crowds at the marinas and the taverns, it attracted many visitors to our region. This is a happy augury for the future of the tourist industry; obviously, fishing in the North Country is a valuable economic resource.

But fishing is more than that. It is a happy avocation. We have a friend who likes to quote what he calls "an old Chinese proverb," as follows:

"If you want to be happy for three days, get married. If you want happiness for a week, kill a pig and eat it. If you want happiness for life, take up fishing."

Among the fishermen gathered here, there must have been members of the Izaak Walton League, a society dedicated to the proposition that fishing is indeed the road to lifelong pleasure and named for a 17th-century English writer. Walton's little book entitled, *The Compleat*

Angler, was first published in 1653. It not only extolled the joys of fishing; it also taught its readers how to achieve the greatest success at this sport. Later editions instructed young anglers how to tie flies but this section was contributed by a friend of Walton, for he confessed he could never master that art. Izaak himself preferred live bait, and he has been widely quoted for his advice about the fisherman's obligation to the creature he uses as bait--a frog or a worm:

"Use him as though you loved him, that is, harm him as little as you may possibly, that he may live the longer."

Walton did not confine his writing to fishing but perhaps coincidentally the men whose biographies he wrote were all fishermen as well as poets, philosophers and statesmen. The *Encyclopedia Britannica* says, "All these subjects were endeared to the biographer by a certain gentleness of disposition and cheerful piety."

These are qualities we like to attribute to fishers, men, women and children. We expect of them that they will love the natural beauty of our waters, mountains and valleys, and that they will strive with us to preserve our environment.

The Izaak Walton League has a remarkable record of active campaigning for protecting the purity of our lakes, ponds and streams.

We hope those fishermen who are not members of the League will be equally active when they return home. We can use their assistance in the drive to persuade Congress and the Administration in Washington to take steps now, not far in the future, to curb acid rain and save our remaining lakes from that fish-killing, polluting fate.

Eastward in Eden

From yon blue heavens above us bent
The gardener Adam and his wife
Smile at the claims of long descent

Thus Alfred Lord Tennyson wrote in 1840. He continued a tradition that linked the English love of gardens with the Biblical Garden of Eden. Sir Francis Bacon preceded Tennyson with his essay on gardens which declared: "God Almighty first planted a garden eastward in Eden."

Such are the credentials which suggest that now at midsummer our gardens will enable us to escape the perplexing problems of a two-hundred-billion dollar deficit that will not go away and an international conference on human rights that found no answer.

Birdsong has been muted as the adult birds no longer worry about territory or proper mates and watch, perhaps proudly, their fledglings enjoy their wings and forage for themselves.

Below the trees the gardens made by men and especially women decorate our world. The fiesta of flowers which began in early spring with the lilac and the shadblow proceeded through roses on splitrail fences, to columbine, coreopsis, loosestrife, salvia, ageratum, petunia, marigold, pinks, shasta daisies, foxglove, lupin, or balloon flowers... we shall run out of space before we exhaust the list. But now in midsummer, they are almost all in their glory, and especially the hollyhock whose blossoms start low on the stalk and will flower at the tip when August merges into September.

There again, the garden has a future, because late August brings the asters, the cardinal flower, and, of course, the hundred varieties of goldenrod.

We in the North Country are fortunate that with our short growing season, nature has contrived to promote the growth of our vegetation at so rapid a pace.

Our gardens know this. The Colonial Garden in Elizabethtown which began in 1957 as a gleam in the eye of the late Ira Yonker, has since delighted the eye of residents and visitor alike, thanks to the Essex County Historical Society and the ladies of the Essex County Adirondack Garden Club. And thanks, too, to Amy Ivy, the young horticulturist who tends the plants and Tom Maxwell who produced them.

There is a reflective, almost sad, note in our enjoyment of midsummer August because we realize that the September frost is not far away, and that bright flowers turn to seed, and the days of sunshine grow shorter with each passing twilight. But we should gather the rosebuds while we may, as the poet Robert Herrick advised three centuries ago, and think now about what we should plant in next year's garden, eastward in our own special Eden.

Nature and Sex

A reader suggests that my columns on nature reveal a preoccupation with the sexlife of the birds, fish and insects, and thus of sex in general.

My answer is that if you study the lower forms of animal life, you will find that they have only two activities, eating and reproducing.

Members of the human race are, of course also motivated by these two urges, but since in developed societies they are relatively easily satisfied, *Homo sapiens* can occupy himself with less basic matters. He can speculate on religion and the nature of the universe. He can spend time on philosophy or science, or in creating music and art.

Plato wrote about these subjects and dismissed all bodily functions, including sex, as beneath the attention of thinking men who should be concerned only with the good and noble. This may have given students of the age the impression that the classical Greeks were superior to such mundane matter as eating and reproduction.

But that is misleading. The people, as distinguished from the philosophers, revealed what they really found interesting in their reverence for gods whose characters had a notoriously venal side. The gods and goddesses feasted on ambrosia, imbibed amphorae of wine and cohabited even with mortals. The morals attributed to the gods of Olympus in their mythology must have seemed acceptable to the people in general.

It took Epictetus and the Stoics an entire century to establish the principle that the good life required controlling such earthy appetites. It may seem to some, however, that the great art produced by the Greeks, the sculpture and the temples, which flourished during the era of earthy appetites, may have actually been inspired by these very human appetites.

We may be doing an injustice to some lower forms of animal life when we suggest that they have no capacity for activities beyond the two cited basic urges.

The social insects, the ants, wasps and bees, for example, have an organized society in which many of its members toil unselfishly for the good of the insect community. The worker bee, for instance, is a female devoid of hope of sex. She gives her life to her tribe, leaving the joys of sex to the male drones and the queen. Reproduction and the survival of the species are extremely important to the bees, however, and they further it each in accordance with the genetic program they have inherited.

And there are other animals, somewhat higher on the evolutionary scale, whose capacity for thought we as yet cannot know. Perhaps some day we may learn that the whales and dolphins have done a lot of thinking about their relation to the universe and to other species. That will require that we improve the means of communication between us and them, in which case they may teach us more than we can teach them.

Note: The sex life of birds can sometimes be as kinky as that of humans. I have read that homosexuality has been observed among pigeons. And the habits of the brown-headed cowbird are scandalous. The female has been described as living the life of a camp follower, the word coming from Civil War times when female prostitutes practiced their trade on the edge of troop encampments. In contrast to the monogamy of most birds, she is promiscuous. She lays her eggs in the nests of songbirds, whose nestlings, being smaller than hers, are often shortchanged on food and sometimes are rolled out of the nest.

Bird Symphony

Here in the Adirondacks on the shore of Lake Champlain we should place a star on our calendar for the middle of May as the lead season for birdsong. On a crisp, sunny morning we should be grateful, especially those of us whose eyesight is failing, for that chorus of song from the throats of what we call our feathered friends.

Nothing compares with the rather sad melody of the white-throated sparrow, which Roger Tory Peterson, the best known of our ornithologists, tells us our earliest settlers translated "Old Sam Peabody, Peabody, Peabody." John Burroughs called the white-throat the bird of the Adirondacks.

The melancholy melody of the white-throat does have something in common with the phoebe's song, which is a two-note transliteration of its name, and with the three notes of the chickadee's mating song; the white-throat's song expands it into at least six syllables.

Then there is the song sparrow and, most musical, the Baltimore oriole whose name the professors have changed to Eastern oriole.

The robin clucks like a barnyard hen most of the day but its vesper song at sunset is heavenly music.

There are many reasons why birds sing, we are told -- to attract a mate, to send a message on the location of the nest, to defend its territory, perhaps to announce the presence of food when flocking, to encourage fledglings to venture from the nest, and to mislead possible predators when the young ones are vulnerable.

There are many other songs for which we need Mike Peterson or other Audubon Society experts to identify. They add to that symphony, all the more to be valued because, like our shadblow, trillium and lilacs, we know they will not last the summer.

The symphony does not end with a crash of the cymbals. Simply the songs are no longer there. This was brought home to me at a little tea party at Croton-on-Hudson many years back, at which two of the "Gibson Girls" were my fellow guests.

These two ladies were the daughters of Charles Dana Gibson, famous at the turn of the century as the masterful illustrator whose drawings for such magazines as *Life* and *Colliers* preserved the spirit and style of the times. For models he used his two daughters, still handsome when I saw them at the tea party.

One of them (was it Lydia?) said "Have you noticed? The birds have stopped singing."

It struck me suddenly that this was true. I noted the date. It was July 15.

So today I prize the middle of May as the season for the songs of the birds, and I am grateful to the Gibson Girl for the warning as to its brevity.

The Hedgerow, Nature's Workshop

We mow our lawns, plant our fields, cultivate our gardens but a narrow space along the fence line we leave to the random exercise of nature. This is, to most of us, wasteland, which we ignore or deplore for its failure to provide any return in dollars or satisfaction for the taxes we pay on it to the county.

Acutally, these hedgerows serve us far more generously than we usually recognize.

I walked our hedgerow this warm and muggy July morning to inventory the vegetation which at this season is abundant. There is chicory already in bloom, goldenrod and aster, which will flower later in the summer. The vines of wild grape and Virginia creeper have created a tangle, tying a lot of the vegetation in a mat of green. There are several teasel plants, now flowering, exhibiting those cones which, when dry, served our grandmothers for carding wool.

Perhaps more important in the long run, there are a dozen young elms, now six to eight feet tall, and several young shagbark hickory trees, originating from the nuts squirrels have carried from the mother hickory on the roadside and buried in the protected undergrowth of the hedgerow.

Among the herbaceous plants along the hedgerow, there are seeds that attract birds, and thick foliage which is fine for nests for birds and concealment for dens of small mammals.

The most important gift of the hedgerow to us is its propagation of the elm seedling. With our mature elms dead or dying from Dutch elm blight, and the species as some predict, doomed like the chestnut, forestry scientists look to each young elm with hope, and perhaps a prayer, that somewhere, sometime, there will emerge an elm with immunity to that blight. Perhaps not. But the hedgerow is nature's own turf, it is her laboratory for experimenting, for trial and error, for perpetuating vanishing species and introducing new ones.

My hedgerow will be here when the 21st century dawns and will provide a bounty for the generation of people and wildlife that comes after mine. Let us hope that an elm immune to disease is among them.

The Pugnacious Ruby Throat

The smaller the creature, the more numerous is the species. This is fortunate because the small ones are prey to large ones and must develop special strategies to survive on an inhospitable planet.

The ruby-throated hummingbird is reputed the most pugnacious of all avians, but he is also agile and swift, and an acrobat and gymnast who, when he cannot bluff the predator, can escape easily from his attacker.

I use the masculine pronoun because it comes naturally when the species is named for the male, the sex that has the metallic red throat. Is this because the early ornithologists were male chauvinists? (*Homo sapiens* is identified as mankind although the better half of our species is female.)

The hummingbird is very much aware of what is called the territorial prerogative, the exclusive right to specific turf. At my hummingbird feeder, filled with a bright red mixture of sugar and water, two pair seemed to fight for a week for property rights, until one pair was apparent victor and the other disappeared.

The hummingbird nest is smaller than a teacup and is usually camouflaged with lichens. John Bull puts egg dates as May 21 to August 16; nestlings June 24 to September 4; fledglings July 12 to September 30.

The female lays two eggs and the young, when hatched are the size of a honey bee.

The hummingbird breeds as far north as Canada but winters from Florida south to the more tropical climes, obviously having the necessary strength to breast the elements for thousands of miles.

Up here the male arrives first, the female following within days, and mating is an acrobatic performance. The male flies straight up in the air, then down, then like a pendulum swinging forty feet in one direction then forty feet in the other.

Those of us who observe the hummingbird see the needle-like bill but seldom, if ever, the tongue. But it is that tiny organ that pollinates some tube-like flowers that otherwise might live infertile lives. This includes the wild columbine, the cardinal flower, bee balm, coral honeysuckle, jewel weed and others.

The young are fed by regurgitated nectar from the mother.

The male devotes little time to the domestic chores. The female builds the nest, sits on the two eggs, while the male perches on a twig, gorges himself on nearby flowers and chases other birds, including hummingbirds, from his territory. Although the pair will return to the same spot next spring, the bird watchers say she will probably build a new nest.

The Media and the Environment

Perhaps we all have our moments of pessimism.

But if we didn't believe that we can change the environmental attitudes of a majority of the people, we don't belong in the business.

We must take into account, of course, the most stubborn and persistent anti-environmental attitudes, those so deeply rooted through self-interest or tradition, or institutions, that progress is disappointingly slow.

Some of these are:

1. The fact that preserving and enhancing the environment is costly. To do the job as it ought to be done could cost as much as the Vietnam War, and while many of us believe that money would be better spent for this purpose, the taxpayers are slow to reach this conclusion.

2. The fact that population control and zero growth is the vital key to the good life on this planet.

3. The fact that land use control and other restraints on traditional individualism, limiting what used to be regarded as sacred property rights, are necessary.

I believe that the people will eventually accept these unpleasant facts if we environmentalists do our job. I am an optimist and the prophet I hail is Rene Dubos. "Unlike animals," he wrote recently, "man can and often does reject consciously techniques or habits that he acquired and social attitudes to which he had been conditioned."

"In fact," he wrote, "his proneness to alter or abandon certain ways of life greatly accelerates or makes possible certain revolutionary changes and thereby sets him apart completely from the rest of the animal kingdom."

His conclusion was: "The crusade against the degradation of life and nature is facing great handicaps, but it can succeed if enough bold spirits really believe that the time has come to convert our industrial society into a humane civilization."

I think we can effectively use the media to argue our point. The magazine, *The Conservationist*, operates on this premise and its growing circulation is a testimony to the increasing awareness of the people, the increasing concern of the people, as to the problem.

But my thesis is that we can be most effective when we avoid the overtly didactic. People resent being preached at. And they are not likely to pay their money for a magazine which makes them uncomfortable or distressed.

Four years ago, when the New York State Conservation Department was reorganized to include the environmental responsibilities of other departments, the staff of the magazine conscientiously attempted to reflect this broadened responsibility. For several issues there was a surfeit of articles on pollution of all kinds, illustrated with depressing pictures of litter, clutter, smoke, smog, sewage, and solid waste. The decline of our circulation was dramatic. Thus, it did not take long for our editorial staff to realize that declaiming a truth is useless if there are no ears to hear it.

We learned that we could more effectively spread our message if our approach was positive. Expressed simply, this meant that a color photograph or a painting of a beautiful Adirondack lake constituted a more effective editorial on eliminating litter than did a picture of litter.

I am over simplifying the lesson deliberately, for what I have to say is more subtle.

If we wish to select from our reading those books which we believe have given us the most profound awareness of our environment, what would they be?

My memory goes back to Ernest Thompson Seton's books for boys, *Two Little Savages*, for instance. This described a summer two boys spend in the woods trying to live as the Indians did. It includes Dan Beard's books, which taught us campcraft.

As I grew older, there was Thoreau's *Walden* and the many volumes of John Burroughs and John Muir, and later the *Sand County Almanac* of Aldo Leopold, and the books of Edwin Way Teale.

The list can be very long and each of you will have your own list. What is common to all of them, however, is that the values of these writers made an imperishable impression on one. The essence of these values is that man's happiness and, we may add now, his survival, depend on his living in harmony with nature.

This is the philosphy or way of life we want to communicate to the people, and we are without the necessity of spelling it out explicitly, I believe. I suggest that if these are our values, what we write, what we paint or photograph, what we film, what we produce in the media, will communicate these values to the people.

Addressing myself specifically to print media, I think we are very fortunate that four color reproductions have been developed in quality to such an extent, and have decreased in cost so much, that printed environmental literature has become many times more effective than just a few years ago. We can reproduce in our magazines the art, in full color, of Audubon, contemporary nature painters, Tail, Winslow Homer and the Hudson River School. These are painters who have made magnificent contributions to the awareness of natural beauty. Their values are implicit in their work. I think we can invoke them to impose the environmental values which concern us on the readers of our print media.

I also believe we can invoke the memory of naturalists like Thoreau, Muir, Burroughs, Theodore Roosevelt and Seton.

Environmental values are not narrow. We environmentalists can say with the philosopher that nothing human is alien to us, and I believe our literature should reflect this breadth of interest. I do not believe we will succeed in communicating our environmental values to the people unless we respond to all their interests.

I am not discounting some plain talk about environmental problems, but I confess that one of my most rewarding chores is the production of the bi-monthly editorial in which I try to deal with such fundamentals as the gloomy forecasts of the Club of Rome, the population explosion, the human priorities in the energy crisis, the environmental ethic versus the profit yardstick of the marketplace, etc. But I would be kidding myself if I thought my editorials would sell our magazine. The editorial plain talk is hitchhiking on the pleasant, enjoyable informative illustrated pages which have given us 185,000 circulation and which I anticipate will continue to increase during the coming year.

* Talk delivered at Cooperstown in 1975 when I was editor of *The Conservationist*.

Strange Animals That Thrive on Poison

Scientists seem to have more fun than most of us because life for them is a series of exciting puzzles. No sooner than they solve one, they encounter another. In high school we learned how plants purify our air by taking in the poisons, the carbon-dioxide, and emitting the oxygen living animal organisms must have. We learned how dependent life is on the sun which acts on the chlorophyl in plants, produces nutritious vegetation which animals, including us, consume for survival.

In recent years, however, the scientists have discovered life that survives without sunlight, fattens on what we always thought were poisons, and prospers at temperatures believed too hot for any form of life.

Strange marine life forms were first discovered in 1977 around geothermal vents in the deep ocean, deriving their energy from the hot water rather than from the sun. They thrive on sulfur, which elsewhere on this planet, as in acid rain, kills fish and stunts the growth of trees and other vegetation.

Now, according to a report in the magazine *Science*, similar organisms, but smaller, have been discovered in sewage outfalls, swamps, marshes and shallow coastal waters. They apparently include bacteria, clams, mussels, tube worms, abalone and some species of fish.

As Sandra Blakeslee reported in *The New York Times*, marine biologists were baffled at how animals survived there without sunlight, with no significant amount of food dropped from the surface and nourished on "highly toxic sulfur compounds." The key to understanding this weird ecosystem, she said, lay in the ability of special sulfur-metabolizing bacteria to support life in the hot water, up to 450 degrees Fahrenheit. The bacteria use energy from hydrogen sulfide to reproduce and grow. The animals simply eat the bacteria.

Comment about the significance of the discovery has included suggestions that it opens the possibility that life may exist in similarly "hostile" environment on other planets.

No one, so far, has suggested that the discovery may offer hope that *Homo sapiens* could evolve in the next million or so years so that we could, as the human race, co-exist with acid rain and other toxic material in our planet. Sometimes we suspect that the Government, which is always finding an excuse to delay action on acid rain, may be waiting for just this evolutionary development.

It is, however, an exciting voyage into the world of *Star Wars* and the *Return of the Jedi*, to speculate on the possibility that having failed to control the toxic contaminants of our planet, the human race evolves to continue to exist even in so inhospitable an environment.

Would human anatomy change to adapt to the new environment? Perhaps with all the lead taken into our bodies, our feet would become heavy. We might even develop little wheels like the robots shown in the space-age TV programs. Because dust from nuclear explosions would have created a curtain across the skies, dimming the sun and depriving us of its beneficient light, we might grow long tentacles, like some plants, to catch more of that light. Around what we now call our face perhaps we would develop something like a gas mask with a long elephant-like snout to protect our lungs from the noxious gases surrounding us.

For those of us who so much admire the present appearance of humans, this is not a pleasant prospect. We would miss the beauty of Venus de Milo, or of Michaelangelo's David, or the Playboy centerfold.

Considering how many milleniums it took for the physical beauty of our race to reach this perfection, we probably shouldn't worry about so distant a future. But on the other hand, wouldn't it make more sense if the government and such agencies as EPA stopped their foot-dragging and proceeded to act to stop acid rain and speed up programs for clean air and pure water?

The Spiderwort Alert

Of course, we all know that the human race is indebted to plants for food and fodder. We also know that our ancestors of merely two or three generations ago attributed medicinal value to certain common plants and wildflowers and some of these old remedies have been scientifically vindicated. The white hellebore, a member of the bunchlily family, is dug commercially for use as an insecticide. Some of us plant marigold between our tomato plants because it produces a scent that tomato bugs dislike. And there are some carniverous plants like the flycatchers that attract insects and then eat them.

But the most surprising of benefactions to humanity from a plant is the ability of the spiderwort, an unobstrusive blue flower with leaves like blades of grass, to warn us of the presence of radio-active material. It can also detect pesticides, auto exhaust and sulfur dioxides, a chemical found in acid rain.

This unique capacity of the spiderwort was discovered by Dr. Sadao Ichikawa, a geneticist in the Saitama University in Japan. When exposed to even moderate amounts of radioactivity the cells on hairs on the stamen of the flower change from blue to pink.

The movement opposed to constructing nuclear power plants has adopted the spiderwort as its official flower and its members are planting this flower near nuclear installations. However, Dr. Ichikawa is studying the plant mainly to determine whether radioactivity influences its genetic development, which may in part answer the question as to the effect of radioactivity on future generations of mankind.

Midsummer Review

Here we are in the first days of August and the leaves of the staghorn sumac are beginning to change color. On the lower branches, the various shades of red and yellow appear, a reminder of the brevity of our northern summers.

For most of our vegetation, of course, there is another six weeks of growing season. But many varieties of wild flowers have come and gone. The dandelion is a pest but like the hepatica, the skunk cabbage, and the showy trillium, it is a promise of spring.

When the day lily blooms in June it is the consumation of summer. But so quickly it passes, leaving us black-eyed susans, the daisy, the blue chicory and the white Queen Anne's lace. In Louisiana the roots of the chicory are ground and used as a substitute for coffee or as an adulterant which gives New Orleans coffee its strong, bitter flavor which the natives like. Queen Anne's lace is a member of the carrot family and I've read that in Europe it was cultivated until our garden carrot was developed.

My favorite is the cardinal flower, the *Lobelia cardinalis*, which is beginning to bloom in moist ground along our streams. It is a brilliant red and usually catches your eye even if surrounded by the green stalks of goldenrod and asters.

But the cardinal flower is an annual which dies after it blooms and depends, I think, on its own small almost powdery seed to come again next summer. The book says that if the stalks are cut back before the seeds mature it will produce perennial, leafy, basal shoots.

In any case, the cardinal flower is so rare that it should be protected.

The milkweed is beginning to flourish with its special promise of maintaining the monarch butterfly population. It will be joined later by the asters, the New England aster with its showy purple petals and its golden carpet. The New York aster tends to be less purple and more lavender.

There are more than a hundred varieties of goldenrod and only an expert can identify them. But we can all enjoy the gold on our roadsides and in our meadows.

By then the sumac will have completed its cycle and we will awake after the early frosts to see the splendid fall colors of the maples, oaks, birches, and aspen.

FALL

Not yesterday I learned to know
The love of bare November days

Robert Frost

A Labor Day Reverie

This, the day summer ended, superficially seemed little different from those that preceded it. Yet, sitting in the warm afternoon, under the birch and white oak I planted as seedlings fourteen years ago, I could sense some changes proceeding around me of which Nature's creatures were probably more aware than I.

The birdsong which beguiled us during spring and earlier summer was silent except for an occasional blast of sound from bluejays and the distant cawing of a crow. Both of those sounds will become more familiar as the jays and crows flock for the community which they, like the chickadees, will form for winter foraging and, perhaps, companionship.

On the roadsides, the goldenrod and Queen Anne's lace are in bloom, the latter already going to seed in those contrived matted balls, so different from the flower. In the flower beds where the perennials dominate, the New England aster is in bloom, in anticipation of the monarch butterfly which feeds upon them just prior to their flight to the butterfly trees in Florida, California or Mexico.

Indeed, it is the insects which exhibit most activity in preparation for winter. The leaf-rollers have been busy for more than a week preparing the nest for their eggs, and they are ripening late. Probably this is due to the heavy rains we have had this summer.

With all this moisture our vegetation is now so lush. My tamarack has cones that hang on the branches and are already turning brown.

The air is full of very tiny flying insects which tax my knowledge to identify. In the sunlight one can see some of them trailing a long thin skein, visible only for a second, with which a web like that of a spider will be contrived, a nest for their microscopic eggs, I suppose. This is probably a community project, like that of the tent caterpillar.

The latter have established their tents on our lilac and crab apple trees, but they were easy to spot and destroy, saving us a lot of defoliation next year.

The cabbage white butterfly, which was unusually scarce this spring, is now abundant. Since they live only two weeks, we can understand their frantic mating as fall approaches.

In the vegetable garden, after an enjoyable harvest of strawberries and raspberries, we now await the ripening of the tomatoes. Twelve seedlings, propped from the ground by Jackie Pedro's well-built frames, now promise a crop large enough to supply a Campbell soup factory. My young pines have grown at least two feet this summer. My apple trees with fruit are bending down, thanks to nature and to a famous apple expert named Emerson James of Peru.

Thanks also to the plentiful rain, my brook which has sometimes gone dry in August, is fast flowing this year and this afternoon I saw a fish, about eight inches long, making an effort to leap the little falls and reach spawning gravel higher up the mountain. For years the brook has been without fish.

Sooner than we wish, the swallows will gather using my telephone line as a staging area for the journey south. There will be a burst of color in the woods and winter will close in. This is sad but not depressing. As long as we live we have a future. I think mine will be to be remembered not for what I have written, but for the trees I planted. They are certainly more permanent than ephemeral newsprint.

This Is Bear Season

The black bears are coming down from the mountains to feed on the corn still standing in the fields or to raid the hives of bee-keepers. The bears pop out of the woods on our road at misty early morning or near sunset, an exciting reminder that the time lapse from pioneer days to the present hasn't been all that long.

The early bear season in the Northern Zone, as set by the Department of Environmental Conservation, began September 17 and runs until October 13. But we have variable bear seasons. For bow it began

September 26. For muzzle-loaders it will be October 14; for regular firearms, October 22. There was even a bear-dog hunt last weekend.

The department isn't worried about maintaining the bear population in the Adirondacks which, it says, is stable and has been so for several years. DEC estimates the bear population in this region at 3,600 which could sustain an annual removal of 800. Hunters' harvest however was 510 in 1981 and 621 in 1982.

The life history of the black bear, although mainly of interest to bears, may be useful to know. The mating is early summer and the young arrive after about 200 days when Mother Bear is safely ensconsed in her winter den which she enters in late November. Bears sleep a lot in winter but they are not true hibernaters. The newborn cubs, two or three in a litter, are no larger than kittens but they grow fast, weighing 65 to 75 pounds by the first fall. They den up with the mother during the first winter and are mature enough at two years to fend for themselves. Father bear is definitely a male chauvinist, accepting no responsibility for the young, and if he should hang around the female's den, she would probably chase him off.

More than any other animal, bears develop bad teeth with lots of cavities, attributable, biologists say, to their liking for honey and other sweets.

John James Audubon and the Reverend John Bachman, who wrote the original text for Audubon's book on American animals, believed the black bear was a heavy meat eater, devouring the farmer's pigs, lambs, calves and even cows. Whether true then or not, today the bear's main fare is berries, nuts, apples, mast, and wild honey when available. Garbage, in the town dump or at campsites, is a delicacy not to be overlooked.

There is considerable variation in weight according to sex. The two-year old male will weigh 200 to 250 pounds compared to 150 for the female cub. The older male can reach 500 pounds, the female about 300.

The male starts his sleep later and emerges earlier than the female, roving about the woods as early as late March, but he may not have a proper den, simply stretching out under cover of bushes and shrubs or even on bare ground in woods. The female wants a more cozy den to protect her young.

Female bears usually stay within ten miles of home but the male roams farther. The Audubon book cites one old fellow that traveled 80 miles in search of food or sex. They are good swimmers and good fishermen. They can climb trees, run as fast as 30 miles an hour and jump up to eighteen feet.

Bear skins were once prized in England and Russia for the fur used to make busbies, the tall full dress fur hats worn by elite gentlemen. In 1803 we exported 25,000 bear skins to those countries which must have depleted our supply of black bear for a while. Bear grease was once believed to have the power to restore hair to bald heads. But let's not let that story get around or we shall see the black bear go back on the list of threatened species.

Chickadees

When we reflect on the blessings bestowed on us by nature, we seldom list the black-capped chickadee whose year-round presence we take for granted. But now, in early October, when birdsong is confined, it seems, to the blasts of the bluejay and the casing of the crows, the chickadees' chickadee-dee-dee is a pleasant reminder of friends we shall have throughout the coldest of winters.

Nature writers always describe the song of the chickadee as cheerful, but that is merely another form of anthropomorphism, a habit we mortals have of ascribing our own emotion to other of God's creatures. Actually we have no way of knowing what is on the tiny mind of the chickadee. At this season, after a summer of raising two families--each with five to ten eggs for a possible twenty nestlings--the chickadees are abandoning their preoccupation with family and gathering in flocks.

Birds are said to sing for two reasons, either as an invitation to mate or to stake out territorial claim. The chickadee has a special call which is related to mating. It is halfway between the song of the phoebe bird and that of the white-throated sparrow, coming out a plaintive phoebe-phoebe. If it really is a mating call, the chickadee is one of the most oversexed creatures we know because that call is heard from late winter into early fall.

About this we do not complain. Mortality rates among birds run high and it no doubt requires a lot of eggs to produce a lot of fledglings, to which we owe the large winter population of the black-capped chickadees.

This survival instinct, to put a nicer name to it, has resulted in some enormous irruptions of the chickadee population in recent years. John Bull said that during three days in October 1954, flocks of chickadees totaling 27,000 were observed near Rochester, flying west to east. In 1961, members of the Genesee Ornithological Society, estimated 42,000 chickadees flew by.

The black-capped chickadee is a benefactor of the human race. He (and she) devour enormous amounts of insect pests and the more you are host to, the less damage you may expect to your trees, flowers and vegetables.

Now in small flocks they are finding insects and seeds in the woods and on roadsides. But when the snow lies heavy and life for them becomes hard, every household should have an outdoor bird-feeder, always filled with seed, including that of the sunflower, plus some suet or good red meat. We owe it to the chickadees to provide something about which they can really be cheerful.

The Bugs of Autumn

If you thought insects were plentiful during spring when the black flies were biting or on summer nights when fireflies were vividly courting in the meadow across the road, sit now in the sun of a warm autumn afternoon.

There is a profusion of flies, wasps, dragon-flies and innumerable flying insects, perhaps an eighth of an inch in size, which would be invisible to the human eye except for their purposeful flitting in the sunshine.

Of these insects only the housefly is really a nuisance. You may swat them, spray them, bomb them, but an hour later they will again be present in force, as if they hatch afresh every hour on the hour. They beat a bass drum on lamp shades; they buzz, and if you nap, they wake you by making a kamikaze dive onto your nose.

It is difficult to understand why nature provided this abundance of bird food when there are so few birds around now to use it. But of course the answer lies in the brief life span of insects. Some live only a few hours. Others a day and very few more than two weeks. (The exception is the cicada which buries its larvae deep in the ground, not to emerge as an adult for seventeen years. But the adult hardly has time to dry its wings because it dies after a week.)

These insects must accomplish in hours and minutes what horses do in 14 months and humans do in nine.

The highly charged activity among these small creatures, then, is vital to their survival. They have so little time to make love, lay eggs, protect the larvae against winter's chill, and provide a new cycle of life to nourish the birds and annoy humans when spring returns again to our latitudes. They have no time to waste.

Harold Morowitz, in his book, *Mayonnaise and the Origin of Life,* tells an anecdote about J.B.S. Haldane, the scientist. Asked by a group of theologians what he had learned from science about God, he responded that the Creator obviously had "an inordinate fondness of beetles." Haldane's point was that God must have loved beetles because he made so many of them. (Abe Lincoln reached a similar conclusion about God and the common people).

Mr. Morowitz informs us that for creatures up to and including one inch in size, there are 740,000 species while of creatures one to ten inches, there are only 20,000 species. Of those ten to 100 inches, the number of species is 1,500. Of those more than 100 inches, only ten species exist.

The tiniest creatures with so little time must work harder than the rest of us merely to survive, but they are highly successful. We suggest that if Washington and Moscow fail in their efforts to control nuclear weapons, and this planet with most of its plant and animal life is devastated, some of those tiny insects will live because they had the good fortune to crawl under a rock and survive the nuclear winter. They will start all over to reconstitute the earth as we now know it. It will take another 500 million years, of course, but it will be worth waiting for. And we will have these small proliferating insects, which we were cussing today, to thank for it.

If there is a moral to be drawn from this little excursion into natural history, it is that world leaders should take a page from nature's book and realize that time may be shorter than they think, even for us.

Salute To The Apple

This is the season we celebrate the apple, not only because it is attractive to the eye, it tastes delicious, it is the delightful ingredient of jelly, pies, and sauce, and its juice, hard or soft, is sweet nectar. No, but because it is also an economic resource to our region.

Frank McNichols, regional extension specialist of Cornell, who helps apple growers in Clinton and Essex counties, says the annual crop of these two counties is worth more than seven and one half million dollars.

This figure can be multiplied by three if we include the jobs which cultivation and harvest generate. Thus, Mr. McNichols says, we are talking about an economic shot in the arm of more than $28 million for Clinton and Essex counties.

New York State is the second largest producer of apples, after Washington State, in the nation. Its annual production is around 25 million bushels, providing a return of more than a hundred million dollars a year to the growers.

Production in Clinton and Essex Counties is about 1,320,000 bushels. Of this, 85 percent will be McIntosh, ten percent Cortland, and five percent Delicious and other varieties.

Figures for cider production are not available. However, Emerson James of Peru, who can press 1,000 gallons a day on his modern hydraulic press, does a land-office business, and is expanding his retail and wholesale sales. There are also many small hand presses which serve the family and go into operation for party gatherings during the season.

Mr. McNichols says our cider business is beginning to feel the effects of foreign competition. Juice concentrates from Europe, South Africa and Argentina, are taking more and more of the market from local producers, he says, but he is cautious about advocating import quotas for fear of retaliation.

The apple has had a charmed existence in our literature, featured in every kind of writing from nursery rhymes to an essay by John Burroughs who describes with some emotion the pleasant sound of a ripe apple falling from the tree in early October. Renaissance painters portrayed the scene in the Garden of Eden with Eve offering Adam a bright red apple. But the apple did not deserve this bad publicity. The *Book of Genesis* did not identify the "fruit from the tree of knowledge." No one can make us believe that we now wear clothes and earn our bread by the sweat of our brow all because of the apple.

The Digger Wasp:
Life Without Mother Love

At this moment in autumn some of our short-lived insects are dying and others, like the monarch butterfly, will soon be departing for their over-wintering grounds in the far South. In both cases, they have left their eggs to hatch, to become larvae and eventually adults.

What is here notable is that these creatures which will emerge next spring, unlike most of the animal kingdom, will never have enjoyed the companionship of a father or known mother love in any sense.

This is not intended as a witticism. It is a fact that has profound significance for the insects that are denied these blessings and for all of the rest of us who are the product of some kind of parental care.

An example cited by biologists of this pathetic life history (pathetic as we see it) is the digger-wasp. You are here referred to Professor Aubrey Manning:

"A female digger-wasp emerges from her underground pupa in spring. Her parents died the previous summer. She has to mate with a male wasp and then perform a whole series of complex patterns connected with digging out a nest hole, constructing cells within it, hunting and killing prey such as caterpillars, provisioning the cells with the prey, laying eggs and finally sealing up the cells. All of this must be completed within a few weeks, after which the wasp dies."

Since there are no parents or fellow wasps to instruct her in the role she must play to survive and to assure the survival of her species, this is not learned behaviour. It is instinct, the product of her genes, her heritage from all the digger-wasps that went before her.

Even the honey bees are more fortunate in that they have the queen bee to provide TLC, the workers to feed them, the soldier-bees to protect them, and the entire hive to teach them how to communicate with each other and how to locate food supplies.

The higher we go up on the scale, the larger are the contributions of the parents to the knowledge of the young. Ornithologists tell us that while birds are especially equipped for the songs they sing, young birds learn much of their song from the adults. Mammals which suckle their mothers to survive and are often fed whole food by a hunting father, have--and probably enjoy--the companionship of the pack. While a great deal of what animals do and don't do derives from instinct, research over recent years attributes a substantial part of their behavior to what is learned, largely from their parents, and from the society of which they are a part.

We humans are blessed with parents which teach us and attend our wants longer than the care given offspring of any other species. Society is also the mother and father of us, and it is because of what we have learned from living, working, playing, worshipping and perhaps praying with each other that we have benefitted so much by science, technology and the arts.

Perhaps we should find a moment or two on next Mother's Day or Father's Day to remember the less fortunate digger-wasp.

The Monarch Miracle

Jane Fonda, being interviewed on the CBS Morning Show the other day, was asked if she believed in miracles. She said she did, and this shouldn't surprise us. Miracles happen around us repeatedly. One that impressed me Wednesday, on a warm, sunny autumn afternoon, was a gathering of perhaps a hundred or more monarch butterflies sipping the nectar of asters and other flowers in our garden.

The monarchs were flocking together for their migration south, either to a specific place in Florida, or Texas, or to the famous pine trees in Point Pinos in Monterey, California. I presume these were bound for Texas or Florida.

They were hatched this spring, from pupae created by larvae, which emerged from eggs laid on some milkweed plants in southern Canada or northern New York state. The metamorphosis, from last autumn's egg to this summer's butterfly, by way of a pupa or sac that hung from the plant, is miracle enough.

But when you realize that these several hundred butterflies in my garden will be joining other flocks of monarchs, all en route to a specific grove of trees which they have never themselves known, you ask: "How can this be?"

Scientists who have studied the habits of the monarch butterfly say it is instinct, something born within them, a driving force which takes them from here to there, to a precise target. But they would also confess that beyond this generalization, they are as baffled as the rest of us. We are justified, I think, to say that something that happens that is beyond our understanding is a miracle.

The monarch has always fascinated those who study lepidoptera. Because their larvae eat the bitter tasting milkweed, monarchs themselves have a bitter taste and birds, and perhaps other creatures, have learned (by experience or instinct?) to avoid them. Thus, free of predators, they thrive, so much so, in fact, that another butterfly, the viceroy, which tastes very good, is saved because its coloring imitates that of the monarch.

In March, the monarchs I saw in our garden on Wednesday will awaken from their dormant period and fly back to the fields and gardens from which they departed in autumn. Back among us, they will mate, find a convenient milkweed plant, lay eggs and die. Their life span is about eight months. But the eggs they lay will become caterpillars which will gobble milkweed leaves, spin a cocoon or pupa, from which another elegant, beautiful monarch will emerge, ready for its eight-month life cycle and its own flight to the protective warmth of the pine trees in Florida, Texas or Monterey.

Tamarack

After the glory of our fall foliage is gone, we still have the bright yellow-orange of the tamarack trees growing on the roadside or further back in swampy ground. The tamarack, or American larch, is the only northern conifer that sheds its needles at the approach of winter.

The tamarack was prized by the early settlers because its wood is hard, heavy, and, being resinous, is almost indestructible. It makes good fence posts, and when tall enough, excellent telephone poles.

E. T. Seton, writing in 1912, said that tamarack fence posts last as long as 20 years. G. B. Emerson, one of the earliest writers on Massachusetts trees, wrote that builders of wood ships sought the timber and especially tamarack roots grown at right angles (over rocky hardpan) to be used as "knees" for joining ribs to deck timbers.

The roots were also made into heavy thread used by Indians for sewing birch bark.

For all this praise of tamarack, I recall one dissenting note. That came from the English essayist, William Cobbett, who lived in America from 1792 to 1800, a brilliant, but opinionated pamphleteer who described the tamarack timber as worthless.

Grouse and rabbits eat the seeds from the small one-inch cones and deer browse on the bark. Further north, toward the Canadian tundra, so the books say, the tamarack grows slowly, but here in the Adirondacks, they reach a height of 80 feet and a diameter of one or two feet.

For most of us, its appeal is its striking color, contrasting with the nearby evergreens and the leafless limbs of the maples, elms and poplars.

The First Frost

The first frost will not catch us by surprise any more than it does the birds. We anticipate it in our bones, which is to say that the expectancy is instinctive, something we have inherited from the millions of years our kind has been alive and evoluting on this planet.

The birds gather in flocks for their annual migration south. If permissable to become a little anthropomorphic, we can imagine them greeting each other: "Good to see you again. How was your summer?" We suppose the older will complain about the necessity of another long, exhausting flight, while those newly fledged this summer will chirp with excitement about the great adventure shortly to begin.

The blue jays and the chickadees will also gather in flocks, but not for travel. They look forward to making it through another Adirondack winter. What do they say to each other? Probably their questions are like our own: "Will it be an open winter, or a closed, icy, frigid one?"

Why they flock is a subject for speculation. Will this help find food or protect them against predators? Or is it merely a human-like desire for companionship?

As for us humans, we may worry about the oncoming season, but each must prepare for it separately. The furnace must be tested, the woodshed filled to capacity, the garden vegetables cooked and preserved in rows of mason jars, apples in the cellar and cider in the fridge.

Winter is not vacation time, but who can deny that after the business of summer chores, we are left with idle hours. Those we will spend at autumn harvest festivals, at church suppers, at community events, at social affairs. For like the birds, we do find flocking together with our own kind a satisfying and necessary activity. And we pause to sympathize with our older citizens, plagued with cabin fever, but confined to home by the difficulties of transportation on days of heavy snow.

Before the snow falls, we shall have the autumn foliage, when nature celebrates in a riot of color for which we mortals should be eternally grateful.

But now it is the first frost which we await. According to the Department of Agriculture's 1941 Yearbook, the average date of the first killing frost is September 11 for Lake Placid, and September 17 for Keene Valley. On the lower elevations of our valley and closer to the warming influence of Lake Champlain, the date is about September 20.

When it comes, the leaves of the pumpkin plant will shrivel and turn brown. The flowers will wilt. The leaves on the maple, ash and poplar will be falling in an ever increasing rain of color and we can wade through them, ankle deep.

Youth, healthy and vibrant, will glory in this season and the winter to come. For them, life is, as always, an adventure and an awakening. For the elders, there is happiness in seeing their children and grandchildren enjoying the spring of their existence. But there is also a touch of sadness, a recognition that the cycles of nature mirror the cycles of life. The first frost declaims the end of a season, but we take comfort in the frost that it thus makes way for another spring and another renewal of life.

Love of Bare November Days

Robert Frost, through one of his poems, taught us to see, in the month of November, beauty to which we might have been blind. "These dark days of autumn rain are beautiful as days can be," he wrote. He talked of "the bare, the withered tree" and the "sodden pasture lane."

Lines in "My November Guest" read:

> *Not yesterday I learned to know*
> *The love of bare November days . . .*

Most of what is green is now brown, except for the pine and spruce. There is still color in the woods, but it is at one's feet, in the leaves which still, for a while, remember the brilliance of their autumn glory.

Even under November's gray skies, one sees farther into the woods, to recognize again, after summer's rich vegetation, the familiar curvature of this rocky land. What is fog to us, as we walk the old logging roads, is mist on the mountain tops. The rains have swollen the brook and the waterfall now reappears, its presence already proclaimed by the sound of its rushing water.

Now is the time to locate the nests in the bare crotches of trees, abandoned households of our summer friends. The bluejays and the chickadees, who are again flocking and now patronize our feeders, need no nests for winter. The squirrels are gathering acorns. If lucky, one can catch a glimpse of a deer under an old apple tree in what was once a pasture.

There is one spot of beauty that is reserved for November, the bright, fluorescent reddish orange of the tamarack tree. The only conifer tree that sheds its needles in winter, the tamarack, stands out against the green of its cousins, the pines, but by December, it will have shed them all and like other deciduous trees, appear only as a pyramid of dark limbs.

But we can treasure it also for its fleeting beauty, for the sudden surprise when we make a turn off the road on a gray November day and enjoy one of the singular gifts of a season which gets less appreciation than it deserves.

To return to Robert Frost:

The love of bare November days
Before the coming of the snow . . .

As if we needed to be reminded that soon what is brown will be white.

Questions Without Answers

What is ironical about nature watching is that he who practices it most faithfully is likely to come up with more questions than answers. Why, for instance, does the witch hazel bloom in autumn, when the leaves are falling, while all the plants we know bear flowers in spring and fruit in fall?

The life cycle of the witch hazel is certainly confusing. The flowers that bloom in the fall have much to do with the case. They bear fruit the following spring, with two black seeds that are forcibly ejected in the summer, and proceed to flower again in September or October.

The twigs, like those of the willow, are reputed to serve as divining rods to locate hidden sources of water. The crushed leaves provide a pleasant smelling balm for men to use as an after-shave lotion.

All this one can learn from a book, but the books don't tell us why. Growth among flora and birth among fauna continue, despite all the books, as miracles which at least to us who are not scientists, do defy explanation.

Why have the robins departed from us so early, while the phoebe is still here? What causes the roses to bloom in such profusion for the second or perhaps the third surge of the season?

Of course we do not need all the answers to enjoy the bounty and the diversity of nature. The speculation and the puzzles could be part of the enjoyment.

Driven By Some Enchantment

Curiosity, not always recognized as a virtue, is undeniably a major factor in mankind's progress from his earliest beginnings; it certainly deserves some credit for his survival in an often hostile universe.

It was curiosity that motivated the explorers and discoverers of all times, even though we cannot completely dismiss the element of material benefit. But whatever the material rewards to the individual, it has been society that gained most.

We cannot all be explorers and discoverers; however, the curiosity in each of us provides an appreciative audience for those brave and hardy souls who searched for knowledge in far places across uncharted distances.

Thanks to television, we of the appreciative audience had a front seat in 1969 when Neil Armstrong and Edwin Aldren crawled out of Apollo II onto the surface of the moon. Our curiosity about that satellite was somewhat satisfied when Armstrong said its surface was "fine and powdery" with no signs of life. For scientists there were the rocks brought back to our planet for more careful analysis.

Explorations into space have continued, of course, aided by unmanned flights collecting data on Mars, Venus, Jupiter and Saturn, while great radio ears listen for signals for intelligent life outside this universe. Credit human curiosity for these magnificent explorations.

Our interest in the findings of Apollo II are no doubt comparable to the excitement in the Old World about the reports of Columbus, Vespucci, Verrazano, Cartier, DeSoto, Coronado, and Champlain.

Not all of these explorers provided records capable of appeasing the appetites of their fellow countrymen for information. Champlain, for instance, was too much involved in using gunpowder against the Iroquois, although he commented that he was astounded by "the vast number of salmon and trout and by the size of the great serpents which seem to infest the waters of both river and the lake." Naturalists suggest his serpents were golden eels formerly numerous where the Richelieu joins Lake Champlain, but some interpret this as the first reference to Champy, the legendary Lake Champlain monster.

An account more descriptive of the New World's flora and fauna came from Jacques Cartier who anchored his two little French sailing vessels off what is now Fund Island, calling it Bird Island because of the enormous number of birds. This was the first description of the now extinct great auk, which served as fresh fowl meat for sailors who had been living on salt pork on their long voyage. In the island Cartier observed the gannets which dive headfirst from 50 feet in the air for fish, and polar bear which sailors killed for food. "His flesh was as good to eat as that of a two-year old heifer," Cartier wrote.

Of the 17th and 18th century explorers and natural scientists, Joseph Kastner in *A Species of Eternity* describes their efforts "as if driven by some enchantment, they went throughout the unmapped country filling bags with seeds, boxes with birds and bottles with carefully killed insects. These they send across the Atlantic to delighted--and demanding-- naturalists who always want more and more."

One of the first explorers with scientific training was Peter Kalm, the young Swedish botanist who had been encouraged to study plant life in America by Carolus Linnaeus, his professor at the University of Upsala who designed the plant and animal classification system followed universally today.

Kalm arrived in Philadelphia in September, 1748, and spent two years living and traveling in Pennsylvania, New Jersey, New York and Quebec province. His mission was to discover useful plants which might be adapted to Sweden for the purpose of improving the agriculture of that country.

Ralph M. Sargent, in a brief introduction to the English translation of Kalm's *Travels Into North America,* writes:

"He was a product of the eighteenth century Enlightenment in Europe, with its quest for information about the world, and its hope for improvement of the lot of mankind." Kalm's journey to America represents a response to the immense European curiosity about the nature of life of the New World and the expectation of gains to the Old World from the land and experience of the colonists.

Kalm did not confine his investigations to plant life, but covered the whole range of natural history. He was enthralled by the ruby-throated hummingbird and his essay on the polecat, which he said was called skunk in New York, is a small classic.

He sent reams of information back to Linnaeus who rewarded him by giving the Latin name for mountain laurel as *Kalmia latifolia.*

Kalm was received with respect by America's own learned men, including John Bartram, the self-taught Philadelphia botanist who was assigned by George III to send to England samples of American plants for the English royal gardens.

Kalm made a special trip to New York State to meet with Cadwallader Colden, a native of Scotland, a botanist, physician, and historian who emigrated to New York at the invitation of then governor of the colony, Robert Hunter. Colden was appointed to his office by the governor and served until 1775 when his advice to England (like that of Edmund

Burke) to conciliate the colonies was rejected. Kalm's discussions with Colden covered a broad range of the ecology of the Northeast. Colden throughout his life in America carried on correspondence with European scientists and men of letters, including Linnaeus who gave the name *Coldenia* to wild heliotrope, a newly recognized plant genus.

Linnaeus was much impressed with Colden's catalogue of American plantlife and congratulated him on his mastery of the Linnaeun system. There was also high praise for Colden's daughter, Jane, who grew up on the family estate at Newburgh and illustrated her father's writing with her own drawings of plants. She was a close friend of William Bartram, John's son, who wrote of his own travels in the Carolinas and the Bahamas. Jane's botanical career, to the disappointment of her English correspondents, ended when she married at 35. As one commentary put it, "botany lost a second Colden."

Colden's letters and papers were published in 1917-23 by the New York State Historical Society. He is especially remembered today for his book on the Iroquois, *The History Of Five Nations,* and for an Adirondack mountain named for him.

There is no question, but that the people have a profound curiosity about the world today and what will be learned about the universe and outer space tomorrow. I suggest that it would also prove profitable to continue being curious about what was learned and reported by those observant explorers and discoverers of the past.

Animal Intelligence

I was walking in the woods the other day with our dog, Suzie, when we flushed a mother grouse and her chicks. The grouse immediately limped off dragging a wing as if injured. This attracted Suzie who took off in pursuit. A few yards along, a safe distance from their young, the grouse winged off, leaving Suzie disappointed and unfulfilled. Both mother and chicks, no doubt soon reunited, survived.

This ruse of the grouse and many other chicken-like birds (gallinaceous is the proper word) is a familiar one; it is only one more example of the kind of animal behavior that suggest to scientists that non-human animals may have a mental capacity far more intricate and complicated than we have previously believed.

I long ago read evidence that crows can count. The story was that ten men with guns invaded a cornfield frightening the crows away and hid themselves. The crows left to perch at a vantage point in some nearby trees. The hunters left their hiding one by one, but the crows did not return to feast on the corn until all ten were gone.

We all know that many animals are capable of warning members of their species as to imminent danger. But I recall when some squirrels I was observing chattered a warning to ground-feeding birds about a house cat stalking in the grass nearby.

Communication between members of the same species, especially the social insects, is well documented. Ants use gestures to tell fellow members of the colony the specific duties they are to perform.

Bees execute dances to inform their co-workers where food is to be found, both as to direction and distance. Scientists say this is given in relation to the position of the sun in the sky and in partly clouded days by use of polarized light.

But a new wrinkle was reported recently by Dr. James L. Gould of Princeton University. In an experiment, Dr. Gould each day moved the food supply from the hive by a factor of 1.25. "He discovered that the forager bees began to anticipate where the food source would next be moved to," *The New York Times* reported, "and that when he arrived at his new location, as far as 3,000 feet from the hive, he would find the bees circling the spot awaiting the arrival of their food."

We know that seagulls drop clams on a tin roof to break their shells; vultures throw rocks at ostrich eggs. Some hawks drown their prey. Wolf packs employ a military squeeze tactic to catch a rabbit or a deer. One of the more fascinating examples of non-human animal intelligence recently reported is that of a heron who patrols the bank of a stream with a feather in his beak. He drops the feather into the water as an angler might cast a fly. When the fish rises to the lure, the heron gets his dinner.

Many scientists are abandoning the theory that all such purposeful activity is instinctive and is programmed in their genetic heritage. They are leaning to the conclusion that non-human animals often are capable of forethought, "of devising a plan and of understanding what the execution of the plan would produce." Intelligence is defined as "the quality of being aware of oneself as an entity in one's environment, and of being able to acquire and retain knowledge, to learn and understand from experience, to solve problems, and to respond successfully to constantly changing situations," according to the *Times*.

The question the scientists ponder now is whether this definition fits some of the surprising actions and reactions students of animal behavior are observing.

So much for communication between members of the same species, but what about communication by animals to humans? Suzie will tell me when she wants to go outdoors (at least most of the time). Some monkeys communicate with use of sign language. Those who train dolphins claim to understand dolphin signals. But we have a long way to go in interspecies communication before we can claim a genuine dialogue.

When that time arrives, a friend says he will get in touch with that heron and ask where he can find the best pool to fish.

Pain

For those of us who have recently undergone an operation, the subject of pain has a fascination. It is largely academic because knowledge of anesthesia has made it possible to protect the patient during what would be a most painful experience.

But paradoxically, the ability to feel pain serves a highly protective function for humans and for most of the animal kingdom. Although Dr. Lewis Thomas who writes a regular column for the New England Journal of Medicine says a dying elm tree feels no pain from the blight, because it has no nerve endings, science may yet discover that plants do have pain receptors.

The classic example of the usefulness of pain to humans is to cite the impulse to withdraw one's hand from fire. Another example, though not often cited, is that the avoidance of pain may keep one from visiting his dentist but the price of that is greater pain subsequently.

It seems that there are two kinds of chemicals found in the human brain--enkephalins and beta endorphins--which are similar to opiates in their ability to affect sensations of pleasure and pain.

Within recent months, some Swedish scientists have discovered through their experiments that earthworms, long believed to be incapable of feeling pain, have these chemicals in the nerves in their cerebral ganglion, which is the worm's equivalent of a brain.

Therefore, it is assumed that the earthworm finds it painful when the angler inserts the barb of a fishhook through its flesh. Thus the worm is closer to higher forms of animal life, including humans, than was previously believed.

But there is also a miracle at work. At a certain level of pain, the pain disappears completely. Lewis Thomas discusses this in a collection of his essays entitled *The Medusa and the Snail*.

He describes a dying field mouse in the jaws of the household cat, a spectacle, he says, which used to make him wince and shout maledictions at the cat for the pain felt by the mouse.

"There are now some plausible reasons for thinking it is not like that at all," he writes.

"At the instant of being trapped and penetrated by the teeth of the cat, peptide hormones are released by cells in the hypothalamus and the pituitary gland (of the mouse); instantly these substances, called endorphins, are attached to the surfaces of other cells responsible for pain perception; the hormones have the pharmacologic properties of opium; there is no pain."

Dr. Thomas muses on the fact that humans have not only pain receptors to prompt them to avoid pain, but hormones which turn off pain when it can no longer serve a useful function. Death comes to us mortals more quietly, more peacefully, and less painfully, than the mourners realize. Dr. Thomas found a similar observation in the essays of Montaigne, which, although based on Montaigne's hunch, coincides with scientific findings 400 years later.

The Woolly Bear

Just as the first robin heralds the coming of spring, the first woolly bear warns of the advent of fall.

Apparently, the first mention of the woolly bear in scientific literature came in 1608 in a book entitled *History of Serpents* by an Englishman named Topsell. He called them "bear-wormes" and said that like Pilgrims, they "doo wander and stray hither and thither."

It is this wandering that brings them to our attention, as they crawl across our driveways or sidewalks or even roads and streets.

The long held belief is that the width of the black bands at head and foot foretell the severity of the winter to come. In October 1958, the staff of the American Museum of History, I hope in fun, collected seventy-four woolly bears on Bear Mountain, measured their bands and concluded that the lack of uniformity among the seventy-four proved that the myth was only a myth. Dr. C.W. Curran, curator of insects and spiders wrote: "The examination of the statistics indicates woolly bears are confused and not at all certain of the winter weather."

The woolly bears are wandering in search of a winter home under piles of leaves or other litter where they will curl up securely until the first breath of spring. Then hunger prompts them to gorge on leaves, building up the fat needed for pupation which follows shortly.

The woolly bear does not appeal to birds or most other creatures, either because of its taste or its bristles.

However, the latter do not deter the skunk which rolls the little caterpillars over in the dirt until its bristles are removed which makes it a tasty meal, at least for the skunk.

If the woolly bear has survived such rigors, it finds a place hospitable for its cocoon between the boards of an old barn, or a fence. After two weeks, the cocoon splits and a moth emerges.

Thus the tiger moth, otherwise know as *Isia isabella*, enters our world. She will mate, lay eggs, and nature's eternal cycle will resume, preparing for another crop of woolly bears to warn us of next year's autumn.

An Autumn Walk in the Woods

This is an odd season but nevertheless enjoyable if one will only put on a heavy sweater and brave the often cloudy and chilly weather for a walk in the woods.

Below your feet is a carpet of autumn leaves, yellow and red, which pick up and reflect the light when a beam of sunlight pierces the mist.

The woods are more hospitable now, more accessible, more knowable, because you can see much further into them. Above, on those trees which have lost their leaves, one can see the deserted nests where the spring migrants built their homes. There are fewer birds about but those which remain are easier to see and identify. There is no shortage of crows and jays, and the chickadee which like many of us cannot afford a winter vacation in Florida, is already chirping cheerfully, perhaps to remind us to keep a full bird-feeder when the seed-bearing plants are covered with snow.

The flickers may have been with us all summer but only now are they truly visible, making noises like the woodpecker family to which they belong, and flashing that white spot on their tails as they dash about feeding on the ground or in the low brush.

Now it is easy to identify the witch hazel, unrecognized and ignored during the summer because its leaves so closely resembled the elm's. But the witch hazel is the only plant which blooms in late fall, and leafless it is there for all to see.

Most of the weeds have gone to seed, a pleasant prospect for grouse and pheasants, but browning goldenrod and aster do not a cheerful picture make. The milkweed pods are breaking open, suggesting, where numerous, a Southern cotton field. The disappearance of so much brush from the forest floor, however, points up the increasing number of white pine seedlings, testifying to the fact that there has been a pretty good "catch" of pine seed during the past several years.

Thanks to September rains, our brooks and rivers are running strongly, but the insects which strode on their surface or flitted just above them are gone, and one doesn't need to be all-knowing to forecast confidently that they, at least, will be back.

One is tempted to describe the present in nature, between the decline of fall and beginning of winter, as a "stasis," which the dictionary defines as "motionless, a condition of balance among various forces."

But this would be incorrect. Despite the appearance of balance and lack of motion, the age-old forces of nature are moving, perhaps more slowly and more quietly, but steadily toward the next arc in the cycle. This, too, shall pass, and under the mantle of snow and ice our world will march to its annual but always glorious rebirth.

THE BETWIXT AND BETWEEN SEASON

Being an essay on the betwixt and between season after Autumn departs and before Winter comes.

The Betwixt And Between Season

Lewis, New York. Chauncey Blinn, our township superintendent of roads, sat in the hall on election day and squinted through the window at the gray clouds. "They say it'll be a tough winter and I believe it," he said.

Leamon Cross, a farmer from over towards Stowersville, nodded glumly. "Can't have it open every winter," he said.

The mood of Chauncey and Leamon is typical of this season in the Adirondacks. It is an attitude of cheerless resignation and is as inevitable at this time of the year as the shortening daylight and the long angle of the sun.

For here we have not four but five seasons. The fifth is the brief period after election day when autumn has departed and winter, with no doubt in her mind as to the certainty of her coming, is content to be vague about the exact date.

There are frosty mornings when the thermometer on my woodshed registers four or five degrees below freezing. But it is not the stimulating, nippy chill of autumn. There is a foreboding dampness about it. The mist which gathers around the peaks of Hurricane and Jay will leave their upper slopes white with snow and there will be flurries before noon if the sun doesn't break through.

But because it is not yet winter, the clouds will usually part and by the time Mrs. Dickerson, the mail carrier on our route, has traversed half of the five miles between Elizabethtown and Lewis, the frost will have melted and everyone (whistling by the graveyard) is saying what a fine day it is.

Of course it can't be a fine day for very long, either. This isn't October; it is well into November. The hope of an Indian summer which beguiles football fans and gay drivers of convertibles a couple of hundred miles to the south, isn't for us. That hope vanished from these parts with the last golden leaf of the aspen in our meadow. Here, at this season, we count it a blessing if the day which was fine at noon hasn't turned wintry by dusk.

So preoccupied are we with preparations for winter, putting up storm windows, laying in fuel supplies, banking dirt and leaves around the base of the house, that we are seldom conscious of the somber beauty which hangs about the mountains, forests and meadows.

The flaming colors are long gone but there is a suggestion of red and gold still in the brown leaves on the forest floor or along the roadside. A ray of sunlight pushing now unopposed into the depths of the woods will lift this color into the atmosphere.

This is the magic moment for the paper birches, and their white bark shines more brightly than at any other time of the year.

In the woods, the limbs of all but the evergreen conifers are bare, and it is now possible to locate the nests of the songsters who eluded you last summer. Near the farm houses, only the tough old apple trees are clinging to their withered leaves. Almost everywhere, the color scheme is brown, but it is a warm brown which remembers, if it does not reflect, the hues of autumn.

There are partridge and grouse in the woods, but around the house the chickadees are taking over. Although there is still food in the woods, they now come each morning and noon to your bird-feeding stations for easy-to-get suet or sunflower seeds. You can take them or leave them now, but in a few short weeks they will be the only sign of life in the vast, white winter.

In the village, the human chickadees who don't go south for the winter, are pursuing their tasks purposefully if not cheerfully. The summer visitors have gone, and with them an important source of our income. It seems too early for the meetings of merchants and hotel operators to plan the campaigns for next summer's tourist trade, and that is fortunate because our seasonal negativism would produce nothing constructive.

The village streets are quiet until three o'clock when the school busses roll through with homeward-bound children. The town comes to life again at five when the final mail of the day is distributed. For a few minutes there is commotion around the post office as cars drive up.

But this is not the season of sociability. Greetings are exchanged without enthusiasm. Someone may mention that it's getting colder. But there is no prolonged chatting in the post office lobby. The box-holder spins the little combination, slams the lid shut and hurries out to his car. Darkness is settling upon the village and as he departs, he switches on his headlights.

The temptations of hunting no longer war with the obligations of husbandry. Our local hunters have either "got their buck" or put away their deer rifles in discouragement. If the woodshed hasn't yet been filled, the rains or snows which make mountain roads impassable will make you regret your tardiness.

A farmer used to figure his fuel needs at fifteen to twenty cords of wood. Since a cord is 4 x 4 x 8 feet, that adds up to a pretty large woodpile. But these days, it's a rare farmer who hasn't converted to kerosene, fuel oil, or bottled gas for at least a part of his heating and cooking needs.

He will still use seven or eight cords for his fireplace and for the kitchen range because the women folk are partial to wood fires in the cooking stove on a cold morning. It takes five eight-inch trees to make a cord, which is another way of saying that for each family, some thirty-five to forty trees must be felled.

This would be a more serious chore if it were not for power-driven chain saws now used to fell the trees and saw them into suitable lengths for fireplace or stove. To fill my shed Red Boyd came over last Saturday after finishing his week's work cutting pulp wood and logs for the lumber company. Red was conscientious about the trees he cut with his chain saw. He by-passed the saleable white pines. He scorned the poplars, "poppies" as we call them, for their poor heating quality. And true woodsman that he is, he chose the dead, or dying, the twisted or gnarled, for my firewood.

Like Thoreau who was warmed first by the splitting of the stumps in his bean field, Red could work up a sweat, even in this damp chill, by the effort of manipulaing the heavy chain saw. Working by the hour, Red determines for himself the timing of his smoke breaks.

Squatting on his haunches, he rolls a cigarette and drinks from a can of beer which he has opened with one corner of his double-bitted axe.

Red tells me that fifteen years ago he left his native mountains in North Carolina to travel with a circus as a roustabout and then as a strong man. During the four normal seasons of the year Red has never doubted his wisdom in settling here in the Adirondacks. But now, with autumn gone and winter approaching, he has doubts.

"It does get pretty cold here," Red said.

At this season there are no optimists.

"Oh, it's time for a real cold winter," 79 year-old Dean White concedes.

Perhaps it will be like 1935 when the thermometer stayed so low for so long that when the mercury reached zero, it was considered a nice day.

"In 1888, I helped my father tap the old Philo Estes sugarbush," says Dean. "The snow was so deep my father had to chop the snow around the maple trees to make a place to hang the sap bucket. And when the snow melted, I wasn't able to reach up to the bucket.

"We used to be snowed in about November 10 to a level of four feet," Dean says. "On New Year's Eve of 1894 there was a thunderstorm for an hour. Then the weather turned off cold and next morning there was eight inches of ice over the snow. The farmers drew their hay to the barn on the ice crust. They didn't bother with gates. They just took the top rail off the fence and drove right over."

As spring is the season of hope, this, then, is the season of premonition, of a sense of impending hardships. It is a time for unending chores, for labor, for resignation.

The mood of the residents will continue through the increasing cold and the countless brief flurries until that magic morning when we awake to find the whole countryside white with the first big snow of the season. The air will be clear and cold. As a people, we will stamp our boots in the snow and briskly rub our hands, and smile at each other with a cheerfulness we haven't known in weeks.

"Isn't it a fine day?" everyone will say.

WINTER

... The hounds of spring baying at winter's traces

Algernon Swinburne

Prescription For Cabin Fever I

The depressed state of the emotions which comes to many of us in the winter is so old and familiar that long ago we knew it as "cabin fever," suggesting that the problem was merely the difficulty of getting out of the house because of the cold and snow. However, the malaise is more complex and widespread. Psychologists say that in winter there are more family problems in the rural areas, like divorce, alcohol-related incidents, and even suicides.

Shakespeare noted this seasonal complaint in the much quoted phrase, "the winter of our discontent."

Science, as so often happens these days, has come up with an answer and a diagnosis. The National Institute of Mental Health in Bethesda, Md., says that many are affected by what it calls SAD, standing for seasonal affected disorder.

The illness affects women more often than men, but for both, symptoms are the same: oversleeping, overeating, loss of interest in work, sex and social activities. Some, it says, become irritable and suspicious.

The cause, they say, is lack of sunlight, and it's true that from the winter solstice, on December 21, to the spring equinox in late March, we are deprived of much of the sun's life-giving rays. We have always known how important that was to plants and to the birds; now we are made even more aware of our kinship to them.

For those seriously affected, the doctors prescribe lots of time under high-intensity, full spectrum electric lights. For most of us, it is a lot more convenient and cheaper merely to put in more time in the sun when it shines.

My own prescription for SAD includes two types of treatment. If we measure winter as three months, Treatment A is for the first six weeks and Treatment B is for the second.

During those first weeks, it is important to appreciate the beauty of winter, which isn't hard to do. The new fallen snow sparkles in the light.

It hangs white over the eaves of the cottage and gathers in the crotches of the leafless trees while it piles up like pillows on the boughs of the pine and spruce.

It is snow that makes the desirable backdrop for the holiday season and one can start by being thankful for the white Christmas. In the woods there is a record to study, of tracks by deer and other creatures. A full bird-feeder will bring you blue jays, juncos, evening grosbeaks and even a few cardinals. Chickadees we have with us always and they are especially welcome now.

For the young there are the winter sports, skiing and ice skating.

After six weeks, however, this routine can pall on you. Therefore, for the final six weeks of winter, we must turn to Treatment B.

That treatment takes its theme from Shelly's lines: "If winter comes, can spring be far behind!"

You will note that this is a statement, not a question. It is the common sense of that statement that provides the hope and the promise that enables one to survive the remaining weeks.

Once in an essay on winter I wrote that the snow that covers the ground is not only the shroud of the season that is dying, but the swaddling clothes of the new season about to be born.

That is the revelation that sustains one in these days when the snow has lost its allure and the chill winds no longer spur one to the joys of sports and exercise. Another poet I like to quote, speaks of the "hounds of Spring baying at Winter's traces." Now come the weeks when one strains his ears to catch even the faint sound of those hounds.

But you do so with increasing success as each day passes, for under that snow and ice the cycle of nature is responding to each additional two minutes of sunshine. The roots of plants are sucking in the drops of water as the snow melts, the buds are swelling a microscopic measure. And that great glory, Spring, is on its way. Of that we can be certain.

Prescription for Cabin Fever II

Mankind is inherently philosophical. That is to say, he instinctively looks for the light at the end of the tunnel. This is fortunate because every year there is winter, and although one can make do with ice fishing, skiing, snow shoeing, and admiring the beauty of new-fallen snow, that season is by definition hardship.

From December 23 the sun hangs in the sky a little longer each day; there is enormous comfort in that. But on the negative side, we have at least eight weeks of cold, snow, ice and slick roads before the first redwing blackbird greets us with his hoarse, but welcome caw.

Obviously we ought to reconcile ourselves to that perspective and make the most of it. For the benefit of our readers aching for relief, we offer the following suggestions:

1. Ponder some of the positive thinking about winter such as we have from the naturalist, Edwin Way Teale: "... in its own way, winter is a time of superlative life. Frosty air sets our blood to racing. The nip of the wind quickens our step. Creatures abroad this season of the year live intensively, stimulated by cold, using all their powers, all their capacities, to survive... Winter provides the testing months, the time of fortitude and courage. For innumerable seeds and insect eggs, this period of cold is essential to sprouting or hatching. For trees, winter is a time of rest. It is also a season of hope. The days are lengthening. The sun is returning. The whole year is beginning. All nature, with bud and seed and egg, looks forward with optimism."

2. Spend some time with seed catalogs beside your fireplace. Plan your flower beds and your vegetable garden. Consider planting some seeds indoors for transplanting later. Think about setting out some white pine seedlings which some 30 years from now will provide merchantable sawlogs for your children. It costs nothing to think about these things and, if the fire is warm, you will even have a sense of accomplishment.

3. If you are young enough or if the blood flows freely in your cardiovascular system, go on the ice of the lake and drop a line. Fresh smelt is

delicious, and, if you are lucky, you may catch other tasty morsels.

4. At the library, borrow a book on animal tracks. The snow provides you with an accurate record of all the animals who last night scampered over this white blanket. When it has gone, the book of animal travel goes with it, and you must wait another year for this chance. Our passion for identifying our fellow creatures is insatiable, and that goes in winter for them as it does in spring and summer for birds.

An Unmistakable Symptom

We stood before the window this morning, my son and I. The thermometer read twenty above, and through the clouds some rays of the sun brightened the view.

"Do you realize, my son," I said, "that once that long white hill was green with grass, that there were leaves on those trees? Do you know that once those flowering crab apple trees were alive with purple blossoms? And let me tell you, once along that red brick walk there were petunias, marigolds, and zinnias. Once that brook, now silent under the ice, did flow making its own music and there was a waterfall just above which sang its own song.

"Just beside that split-rail fence there were rose bushes and a bed of cosmos where hummingbirds came to drink the nectar. Under those trees there were once lawn chairs where people sat in warm summer days with a book or a glass of bourbon."

My son looked at me oddly.

"Father," he said, "your mind is slipping. Perhaps you don't feel well. Sit here by the fire and I will get a robe to throw about your knees. No, father, there has always been snow and ice, and we cannot remember anything else."

There is no moral to this story. It is merely an anguished voice crying out for Nature to move along. A little more quickly, please.

A Bad Guest

One of Mark Twain's more profound statements was that while everybody talks about the weather, nobody does anything about it. But it is precisely because we can do nothing about it that we need to talk about it. As the psychiatrists have taught us, talking about our deep seated problems is useful therapy for the psyche. It may not cure cabin fever, but it makes that very common ailment more bearable.

And this indeed has been our winter of discontent. As Nietzsche said a hundred years ago: "Winter, a bad guest, sitteth with me at home; blue are my hands with his friendly handshaking." The trouble is that winter, like the man who came to dinner, doesn't know when he has outstayed his welcome and should depart.

As winter persists beyond its appointed time, it compounds all our other problems. This is the season when we face up to the demands of the collector of income taxes. It elicits from the Wall Street experts the gloomiest predictions about the stock market. It brings pessimism about Washington's ability to tackle the deficit. And only a President who makes a profession of optimism could see a four tenths of one percent drop in unemployment and ignore the fact that millions of workers are still without jobs.

The poets have struggled over the ages to find for themselves and for us some perspective about the negative psychology of a long winter.

Perhaps the only cure for cabin fever is the memory that winter always ends and is always followed by the joyous season of rebirth and replenishment. If the return of the redwing and the robin is delayed, it is a delay that makes their later coming more exciting. Even under the snow we know that skunk cabbage and hepatica are already green. The buds on the lilacs are swollen, requiring only a slight warming trend to burst into leaf. In the woods, the chickadees are singing their mating song while they flit about the feeders on the leafless trees.

So we all shall sit by our fireside, our hands blue, entertaining that bad guest, winter, but our ears are attuned for the faint baying of the hounds of Spring out there somewhere in the forbidding ice and snow.

The January Thaw

January was named by the Romans for the god Janus, the deity associated with gates and doors who was reputed to have two faces, one looking forward, one looking backward. This is an appropriate name for the month because it does for a brief period face in two directions.

For most of the month, January looks to the cold winds, ice and snow blowing down on us from the north. But at some time toward the end of the month the weather changes its direction. It warms up, the sun shines, the mist sits upon our valleys and decorates the distant mountains. This is the January thaw.

Meteorologists, trained in the science of weather, are loath to recognize the January thaw because there is no scientific basis for predicting it. It just happens, and the fact that it happens every January without fail, does not impress them. But the old weather forecasters for the almanacs know better.

The Old Farmer's Almanac for 1985 (its 193rd anniversary) does not use the word "thaw," but it confidently predicts that between January 23 and 25, we shall have warmer weather and "rain," not snow.

In copies of previous years still at hand, we find that in 1981, the forecaster predicted "rain and mild" for January 25 through 31. In 1977, he was bolder. January 27 to 28, he said will be the "thaw."

People in the North Country take the January thaw for granted and rely on a wisdom older and more profound than the scientific meteorologists performing theatrically on the television screen.

The thaw provides hope after the bitter cold and although it will be followed by more cold and perhaps February blizzards, it fills us with faith that the old cycle of nature from death to rebirth will again repeat itself.

Out in Wisconsin, they also count on the January thaw. In his little book of essays entitled *A Sand County Almanac,* the late Aldo Leopold wrote of one January thaw when the warmer weather aroused a hibernating skunk whose tracks he could follow for more than a mile. Leopold was fascinated also by the tracks of a field mouse and recreated one dramatic moment when a rough-legged hawk ended the career of that little creature.

Which reminds us that the blanket of snow, for all the inconvenience it causes, is a blessing. Leopold recalled that in 1898 a dry fall followed by a snowless winter "froze the soil seven feet deep and killed the apple trees."

We often hear about "the year without a summer" which frightens us, but we would also pay dearly for a year without a winter.

The Mourning Dove

Barney Fowler recently reported in his column in the *Albany Times Union* that legislation has been introduced to end the protection now granted by New York State law to the mourning dove. Some 30 states permit hunting of the dove, but in some, the 12-bird bag limit and the cost of shells, hunters say, makes it unattractive.

Roger Tory Peterson, in his *Field Guide to the Birds East of the Rockies,* has the mourning dove breeding in a small area of northeastern New York, but a resident year round in southern New York and south to the Gulf of Mexico. He acknowledges this situation is changing; he notes that the mourning dove is expanding north in winter at feeders.

We know from personal observation that the mourning dove population has increased enormously in our own time. Thirty years ago there were two or three pair to be seen at the intersection of the Back Road to Lewis and the Cutting Road. Now at our feeder near Reber, in the middle of winter, we can see flocks of twenty or thirty.

This coincides with a national trend observed by the U.S. Interior Department as early as 1966. Comparing Christmas counts by Audubon

Clubs, a department report said that mourning doves increased from an index value of 13,131 in 1949-52 to 59,886 in 1957-60.

This increase has not made the dove a pest and so far as I know, no farmers are complaining about doves damaging their crops. In fact, most farmers are reported opposed to opening a season on doves because they believe it will lead to hunters parking their cars along the roads and firing into their fields when they sight the birds.

For most of us, the mourning dove is pleasant company. Their song is a quiet cooing and the whistle of their wings as they fly off to the pines is a song in itself. The dove early became a symbol of peace, and played a Biblical role when he returned to Skipper Noah with a green sprig in his mouth to announce that the flood was receding.

Doves are constant lovers, clinging to their mates until death. They build very flimsy nests and produce two broods of two eggs a season. Male chauvinism is unknown and care of the young is shared by mother and father. One writer claims that the female sits on the nest from two o'clock in the afternoon until nine or ten the next morning with the male sitting the other four or five hours. "The males feed twice each day, from daylight to about 8:00 a.m. and again late in the afternoon; the females feed only in the afternoon." All the males are said to be back on the nest by 10:00 a.m. sharp. (I am trying to believe this.)

Doves feed their fledglings by pumping up partly digested food into the mouths of the young. This is common to all pigeons and doves and is called pigeon's milk.

John Bull in *Birds of New York State* fixes egg dates as ranging from March 9 to September 28; nestlings April 6 to October 5; fledglings from April 24 to October 26.

There will undoubtedly be widespread opposition to opening a hunting season on doves, partly because people remember the greedy slaughter of the passenger pigeon. Unlimited netting, even during the entire nesting season, eradicated what was an enormously abundant bird. It has been reported that more than a million of them were netted and sold on the market from a single roost in one year. No one wants to see this happen to the mourning dove.

If the legislation described by Barney Fowler is enacted, it is hoped that any hunting permitted will be strictly regulated and the regulations enforced.

The Grosbeaks

If you put sunflower seeds in your birdfeeder, you are no doubt a frequent host to a robin-sized yellow bird with a big beak called the evening grosbeak. There are other grosbeaks--the rose-breasted, the pine, and the blue--but all they have in common is the proboscis that reminds my generation of Jimmie Durante and our children of Corporal Klinger. The Latin names show they are not kin.

They do share preference for the same foods: the seeds of conifers, box elders and other maples, which their nut-cracking beaks easily handle.

To me, there remains a mystery about the evening grosbeak. They were unknown in the Adirondacks and the entire Northeast until January, 1890, when they suddenly appeared in blocks of ten or twenty. For bird watchers accustomed to greeting mainly the neutral-colored chickadees on these frosty mornings, the bright yellow of the evening grosbeaks was exciting.

Ornithologists seemed to have agreed that there had been a population explosion in the evening grosbeak's habitat, which until then was believed to be southern Canada and Upper Michigan. In 1934, a student of birdlife named Magee, operating in Sault Ste. Marie, began banding evening grosbeaks to learn about the migration. He reported that while a few flew to Maine, the vast majority went slightly southeast to the Adirondacks and to Massachusetts and other New England states. In other words, they bred in Upper Michigan and wintered in upstate New York and Massachusetts.

That is no longer true, if Roger Tory Peterson and John Bull are correct. Peterson's map for the evening grosbeak has that bird breeding and wintering throughout the whole range from Upper Michigan to the New England coast. John Bull in *Birds of New York* has the evening grosbeak breeding from south Canada to northern and east-central New York state, rarely to Massachusetts, casually to southeastern New York, southern Connecticut and northern New Jersey. He reports that the bird winters in the northern part of this breeding range.

Mr. Bull says the first summer occurences of the evening grosbeak in this state came in 1942 and 1945, but by 1947 there was evidence that these birds were breeding here. He offers impressive evidence of their breeding, mainly in the Adirondacks, but also in other locations in the state.

In 1961, there seems to have been an irruption in numbers. Bull reports that not only did the grosbeak become more numerous in their accustomed Adirondack habitat, but their range extended far beyond the Blue Line into southwestern New York, Connecticut, Massachusetts, and Pennsylvania.

Sudden population explosions are a mystery, the solution of which may fill in gaps of our knowledge about evolution. Some day we may learn why *Homo sapiens* 35,000 years ago multiplied so rapidly that his species out distanced the Neanderthals and created the culture we know today.

Knowing why, we might then give some thanks for the knowledge of that bright yellow bird which descends upon us each winter in those flamboyant flocks.

About Birch, Rabbits and Forsythia

Two recent items of news are intriguing because, in an odd way, they are related. Their relationship lies in the statement they make on how nature manages and sometimes mismanages affairs in her world.

One concerns the variation in the population of snowshoe rabbits in Alaska and generally in the Arctic circle. For years scientists have noticed that about every ten years, these rabbits reach a peak in numbers, then decline. The new discovery is that this variation is tied to the cycles of growth of the paper birch. New shoots of paper birch contain a resin that makes the birch, ordinarily the favorite food of the snowshoe rabbit, odious and hateful to the rabbit. Other food is scarce in the Arctic wastes and many rabbits die of starvation.

As the birch matures, it no longer contains the resin and the rabbits enjoy it and multiply. In fact, they multiply so abundantly they overwhelm the food supply with the expected result; their population declines sharply.

By thus maintaining the balance between birch and rabbits, nature has managed the survival of both.

Incidentally, the paper birch in our zones does not produce this resin, and doesn't need it.

The other item of interest is that in and around New York City, some spring-flowering trees are bursting into bloom. Botanists at the Brooklyn Botanical Garden, besieged by questions from citizens, explain that for some reason we have had a longer than usual growing season. Spring started early and we are yet to have a hard freeze.

It is not that temperatures have been unusually warm. The answer lies in the internal computer of plants. Their clock or calendar calls for a specific period of dormancy.

Rob S. Coleman, of the Garden, said: "The primary cause seems to be the longer length of this year's growing season. The early spring means that plants which bloom in the spring and then set flower for the following year had a longer season within which to do so. The longer fall season gives these same plants time to bloom before dormancy and winter sets in."

This explains why some of our forsythia plants, ordinarily early spring bloomers, broke out with yellow blossoms just before Thanksgiving.

Tomorrow's forecast promises the freezing weather which the forsythia needs for its belated dormancy.

Some Benefits of Snow

We entered March this year with far more snow on the ground than usual. Even after several days of mid-day thawing, there is at least a foot of it on flat land; plowed driveways and shoveled walks have resulted in ridges four feet high.

It will be interesting to observe how this has affected the growth cycle of our vegetation, something we can watch as warmer weather, until now delayed, banished the rest of the snow.

The lower limbs of the evergreens are still bent in incongruous shapes. Shrubs, such as the bridalwreath, look as if disaster had struck. Large limbs of many white pines have broken off under the weight of the snow, a phenomenon described by a friend as "nature's own pruning."

Above ground, nature appears to be moving on schedule. The pussy willows are budding and the weeping willows, always first to herald the coming of spring, have bright color in their branches and twigs. The lilac buds are larger and if we could examine those of other trees, like the birch and aspen, we would probably find the same is happening to them.

The question which time will answer is the effect of the heavy snow cover on certain perennials. At this latitude, at least on our side of Lake Champlain, forsythia is capricious. One can seldom predict accurately whether we will have the bright yellow blossoms or merely green leaves. In some years, we will have blossoms where the bush has been protected by snow, and the flowers appear only below what was the snow line. But this year's heavy snow has also warmed the roots and it is just possible that for the first of many springs we may have a fiesta of forsythia blooming.

We have had our winters with cold nights and sparse snow. Most of us lose some rose bushes every winter. Perhaps this will prove an exception. We shall soon find out. And we say: the sooner the better.

Creation and Diversity

Most scientists believe our universe began with the big bang, and the creationists who prefer the Genesis version see it as a quiet week's work by the Creator. Recently, the astronomers claimed to have discovered a galaxy ten billion light years away, establishing that the universe, if not our own solar system, was already operating at that time. Their discovery, by coincidence, was occurring while a California court was hearing an attack on the theory of evolution which of course needs an almost infinity of time (at least in terms of hundreds of millions of years) if it is to convince any of us that *Homo sapiens* actually descended from something that crawled up from tepid water onto ancient sands.

But the California report of the Scopes trial of 1925 which started off with a media big bang, ended in a whimper. The creationists agreed that the schools could continue to teach evolution and need not insist that Eve was modeled on a rib of Adam, but would be satisfied if the biology teachers merely informed their students that evolution is a theory that "most scientists believe."

For those of us who were around in 1925 when William Jennings Bryan, the prosecutor, debated Clarence Darrow, the defending attorney, we are confident that the old silver-tongued orator, as Bryan was known, would not have accepted such a settlement. He won his case, and Mr. Scopes, the modest little Tennessee teacher, was fined $100 for teaching that man had descended from lower animals. But Mr. Bryan's victory was pyrrhic--he won a battle, but lost the war. During the 56 years which have followed, scientists have collected impressive evidence to support both the theory that the universe was born of big bang and that life today evolved over millions of years.

At the meeting of the American Association for Advancement of Science in Toronto in January, Porter M. Kier of the Smithsonian Institute presented the fossil record of evolution and said that it could be supported by "one hundred million examples" from museums and institutions around the world.

But science is not so cocksure as this may appear.

The best minds among our scientists and philosophers continue a passionate search for more knowledge about us and our universe. Dr. Lewis Thomas, who writes a column for the New England Journal of Medicine, and has published several volumes of essays, said in his Harvard Phi Beta Kappa Oration that "puzzlement is an identifying characteristic of the human species."

One of the puzzles that bothers him is not the fact of evolution, but of possible facts not yet known.

"I cannot make my peace with the randomness doctrine," he said. "I cannot abide the notion of purposelessness and blind changes in nature. And yet I do not know what to put in its place for the quieting of my mind. It is absurd to say that a place like this place is absurd, when it contains, in front of our eyes, so many billions of different forms of life, each in its way absolutely perfect, all linked together in a form that would surely seem to an outsider a huge spherical organism.

"We talk some of us, anyway--about the absurdity of the human situation, but we do this because we do not know how we fit in, or what we are for. The stories we used to make up to explain ourselves do not make sense anymore, and we have run out of new stories, for the moment."

Freeman Dyson of the Institute for Advanced Study at Princeton who gave the Phi Beta Kappa Public Lecture at the Toronto meeting, demonstrated that he had something in common with Dr. Thomas's puzzlement. He argued for an acceptance of the endless diversity of the universe in contrast to those scientists who would unify it "in a set of equations." Dr. Dyson suggests that the diversity of life in our planet, and in our own cells, is equally infinite.

A contemporary scientist, John A. Wheeler, of the University of Texas, is quoted by Dyson approvingly as another who sees an endless diversity:

"Individual events. Events beyond law. Events so numerous and so uncoordinated that, flaunting their freedom from formula, they yet fabricate firm form."

Dr. Dyson considers along with Dr. Wheeler the possibility that the laws of physics may be contingent upon the presence of life in the universe. Thus, as he points out, life and intelligence would be equal with Einstein's general relativity as factors influencing the universe.

I do not say I understand this completely, but it provokes my mind to look deeper. Dyson told his audience in Toronto that he would be disappointed if the whole of physical reality could be described by a finite set of equations.

"I would feel that the Creator had been uncharacteristically lacking in imagination," he said.

The world of physics is truly inexhaustible and the universe is infinite in both directions. So say Dyson, Wiechert and Wheeler. And, this is what I think Dr. Thomas is saying.

The more one learns, the more he must attribute a subtlety and imaginativeness to the Creator far greater than the beautiful and symbolic poetry of Genesis suggests.

Our White Pine Forests

Twenty-three years ago a young forester who worked for Ward Lumber Company in Jay told me that northeastern white pine was the one tree that was reproducing itself faster than it was being consumed. I do not know whether this is true today. There are some beautiful stands of white pine in Essex County, one of the most notable being the county tree plantation in Lewis, started on the initiative of the late Harry MacDougal who believed that when the timber matured, its sale would save us taxpayers a bundle.

But all our white pine is second or third growth. We do not have the 200-foot logs, six feet in diameter, which used to be reserved for the masts of King George's navy. Logs three feet in diameter are occasionally seen but are not common.

About fifteen years ago, our white pine forests were threatened by blister rust, but once the connection between this disease and currant or gooseberry bushes was known, the state and federal governments acted promptly. Roving gangs of young men showed up and uprooted or killed the offending bushes. Gooseberries are now scarce but our white pines were saved.

In 1947, Wisconsin had to choose between protecting its white pines or retaining an exceedingly large white tail deer herd. Aldo Leopold, who died in 1948, was one of the most admired and respected conservationists in the country, and he was named to a state commission to design policy on the issue. He came out strongly for the pine which he said was being destroyed by the deer.

Leopold said that a white pine seed year, largely dependent on the weather, occurred only once or twice every ten years. If Wisconsin failed to get a "catch of pine" during the decade of the 1940s, Leopold said, it might have to wait a half century for another chance. Leopold failed in his efforts for a reduction in the deer herd but that reduction was later achieved through starvation. As the deer herd was reduced and deer browsing of white pine seedlings curtailed, white pine has apparently made a comeback in Wisconsin.

The favorable factor is the ability of white pine to reproduce itself. Much of Essex County's white pine is growing on what was once farm land, open meadows where the seedlings can get the sun they need. Our soil is the sandy loam the pine loves.

If my observation is correct, a large proportion of our white pines are between twenty-five and thirty years old, which coincides roughly with the period when our farms began to be abandoned.

It is not difficult to estimate the age of these trees. White pine branches spring out in whorls around the trunk at the rate of one whorl a year. As Rutherford Platt says, "you can tell the age of a white pine by counting these worls from base to top." It is necessary to add three for the first year. It can be seen that after the fourth or fifth year, when the root system was developed, the tree grew two and a half to three and a half feet a year.

I have observed sadly that in the white pine trees on our place, there seems to have been a heavy weevil infestation when the trees were about nine years old. The weevil kills the leader and the tree must transform a branch into a new leader, which saves the tree but can spoil it for timber.

The First Frost

This morning, as we write, we look out on the first real frost of the season which is already vanishing as the sun's rays spread out across the fields.

The frost comes as our autumn foliage reaches its peak of high color. Rain and wind may soon obliterate this gaudy show but for the moment, it is here for our enjoyment. Nowhere but in the North Country is the change of seasons so dramatic. It is the perfect example of an old philosophical principle, that quantity becomes quality. This is another way of saying that something remains the same as additional units of heat or cold or time or ingredients pile up until--bam! the thing itself changes into something entirely different.

As the days become shorter and the nights cooler, a layer of corky materials builds up where the leaf stem is attached to the twig. The botanist, E.F. Steffek, describes the process as follows: "As this layer grows it gradually cuts off the supply of cell sap going to the leaf. Consequently the manufacture of chlorophyll gradually ceases and what chlorophyll is left slowly deteriorates."

When this happens, the other substances show through--carotin and xanthophyll for yellow and orange; anthicyanin for red and purple.

Our forefathers believed that it was frost that turned the leaves into these lovely colors, and many of our neighbors still think so. But that illustrates another principle known as the *post hoc, propter hoc* fallacy. That is the Latin for saying that if two happenings occur more or less simultaneously, one must have caused the other. That is wrong, the old logicians used to say. If the rooster crows and the sun rises, that does not mean that the rooster's crow caused the sun to rise. Thus we may dispell the fallacy that the leaves turn because of the frost.

There is enough magic in the process, however, to enchant us all, regardless of philosophy and logic.

In his book, *Autumn Across America*, Edwin Way Teale conceded that "the exact process by which the tide of autumn colors recede and browns of varying shades take place is still imperfectly understood. Tannins, always present in the changing leaves, are believed to play a leading role. Through the whole chromatic parade of the fall foliage all the tints and hues and combinations and shadings are the work of various pigments. But the universal brown that envelopes the autumn leaves at last is rather the product of gradual decomposition of chemical changes taking place little by little."

So the little by little in quantity become a transformation in quality and we are left, after the glory of fall, the sere, sad browns that are the forerunners of a North Country winter. It is fortunate that the trees that gave us the enchantment of color will also give us the comfort of a warm fire on the hearth.

Continuity, Predictability

The earth is now tilting away from the sun and about December 22 the sun will be over the Tropic of Capricorn, far to the south. As I write, on this day, the sun rose at 6:44 and set at 4:17, giving us nine hours and four minutes of daylight, one of the four or five shortest days of the year.

Astronomers call this the winter solstice, and it signals officially the beginning of winter. We have another solstice, on June 22, but this is so far off now, that it hardly seems worthwhile to write about it. The solstice is described as one of the two days when the sun "has no apparent northward or southward motion, at the most northern or southern point of the ecliptic."

However, mankind lives on hope, and although December 22 may be bitter, cold, and dreary, we can rejoice with its coming, because immediately the days become longer, about a minute a day, until that magic day in June, the summer solstice, when daylight lasts fifteen hours and seventeen minutes. Then the earth will be tilted toward the sun, which will be over the Tropic of Cancer.

There will be a lot of exciting things happening before then, of course. March will come in like a lamb heralding the beginning of spring, officially calculated as March 21. March may be wintry and certainly muddy, but there's April on the way, with the budding lilacs straining to bloom, and the first migrant robins plucking worms from the thawing soil. In my own journal, I have marked March 17 as the day I saw my first redwing blackbird. But it is also the day my son broke his leg skiing on wet snow.

But now we have Thanksgiving coming up and sooner than we expect, Christmas Day.

Mankind has known about these details of the solar system since the seventeenth century, thanks largely to an Italian scientist named Galileo Galilei, who proved that the sun did not revolve around the earth but the other way around. He was persecuted by the Church and was forced to recant, but legend has it that he said under his breath: "But still it moves."

A stubborn old man, but he lives on. His spirit was no doubt aboard *Voyager 1* last week when it made those astonishing pictures of Saturn and its moons.

Those who persecuted Galileo are also alive in spirit in those who call themselves Creationists and condemn the findings of science with respect to the birth of our universe and descent of mankind. For me, evolution casts no shadow on the divine origin of us humans. A God who created evolution is no less to be revered than a God who put Adam and Eve in the Garden of Eden. We lose nothing of that reverence in applying what we have learned from that God-given talent of humanity in discovering what has happened on this planet for three billion years.

Northern Lights

One reason that it is better to live in Essex than in Westchester County is that we have a better seat, almost a front row seat, to see the aurora borealis, or Northern Lights.

The aurora, named for the goddess of dawn, is that breath-taking sheet of greenish white light across the northern horizon on certain nights. Ours is called borealis for its northern origin; they have one at the South Pole called aurora australis.

The explanation of the aurora is complicated. It involves the electromagnetic environment in space around the earth. Recent scientific writing has compared the process by which we see the aurora to the television tube. As the *Encyclopedia Britannica* puts it, "the magnetosphere acts like a giant cathode ray tube, generating and acting upon electron beams that in effect produce the image (the aurora) on the gigantic screen that is the polar upper atmosphere."

The source of energy of the aurora comes from the sun, a theory of Galileo's confirmed by modern science. Aurora activity that is generated by solar flares "activates this gigantic cathode ray tube and causes intense auroral display," says the encyclopedia.

This is relevant to us now because the sun is entering a period of great activity. "Big storms are coming," according to a scientist at the Space Environment Services Center at Boulder, Colorado. The indications are that the sun is moving into one of its 11-year cycles which will last for many months characterized by turbulence, rolling magnetic forces, and great explosions that will spew hot gases and intense radiation out into interplanetary space. The flares can affect space vehicles, radio waves on earth, and surges in power transmission lines.

And since the high energy particles thrown out by solar flares can penetrate the earth's magnetic shield, be trapped by the Van Allen radiation belt and deflected toward the polar regions, they will dramatically increase the visibility of the aurora.

Scientists predict as many as 154 sunspots between early November and March.

The prospect is that we will have a historic and unforgettable display of the Northern Lights this winter. Perhaps our chambers of commerce should advertise this as a tourist attraction along with the Olympic Winter Games. For these the front row seat is without charge.

Memorial to the Dodo Bird

If you are looking for a metaphor to say something is really extinct, you say it's dead as a dodo bird. The dodo bird is certainly dead. It was last seen on earth in 1681 on the island of Mauritius off the east coast of Africa. It was first recorded as seen in 1507 by Portuguese sailors who gave it its name, "doudo" which in their language means silly.

The dodo must have looked silly. It was large and clumsy. It could not fly and apparently was unable to walk fast enough to escape its predators, hence its extinction.

Just recently, 300 years after the disappearance of the dodo, scientists have begun to study the last of a vanishing species of tree on Mauritius. Its name is *Calvaria major*. It is a very large tree producing a nut, or seed, enclosed in an extraordinarily thick endocarp.

The *Calvaria major* is dying out because its seed, protected by such a thick cover, cannot germinate.

Stanley A. Temple at the University of Wisconsin suggests that the tree developed this thick endocarp in response to its destruction by the dodo bird. But this was self-defeating because only the dodo bird had a gizzard tough enough to grind the *Calvaria* seed, or to crack it so when excreted it would germinate and produce more *Calvaria* trees.

In any case, when the dodo died it spelled the end of the *Calvaria* tree.

This is not the altruism about which we wrote in a recent column, for neither the tree nor the bird cared a hoot about helping the other. The relationship is called mutualism, an association between two organisms with a benefit to each.

This is happening around us with such frequency that we pay little attention to it, miraculous as it is. The insects drink the nectar of the flower and repay the flower by spreading its pollen. Any student of high school biology could give a dozen other examples. And a student of anthropology could explain how, by domesticating certain animals like cows, horses, and sheep, man assured their survival along with himself.

Professor Temple commented that many instances of plant-animal mutualism are known in which the extinction of the plant species affected the survival of the animal. But this case of the dodo bird and the *Calvaria* tree is the first on record in which the disappearance of the animal resulted in the extinction of the plant.

Perhaps 300 years from now, after the Tennessee Valley Authority has destroyed the snail darter at Tellico Dam, we may discover that the tiny fish played an unsuspected important role in our human ecology.

*Notes on Nature Writing
And Nature Writers*

The Craft Of Outdoor Writing

A friend who writes an outdoor column for a local paper and articles for outdoor magazines, recently asked me to write something about the craft of an outdoor writer.

My first reaction was that the craft of the outdoor writer is the same as for all writers. You do not split infinitives (or hardly ever) and you avoid dangling participles. But the more I thought about it, the more I tended to the conclusion that readers of outdoor writing are special and that satisfying their demands makes special demands on an outdoor writer.

In the first place, an outdoor writer could not get away with the sentimentality so cloying in some of the nature poets of the mid-19th century. Take Shelley's "Ode to a Skylark," which begins, "Hail to thee, blithe spirit, bird thou never wert." Translating that into normal English, it would read, "Hi there, light-hearted spirit, you never were a bird." This may be good poetry, but it is pretty weak outdoor writing.

I can remember equally sentimental nonsense from Wordsworth. He wrote that looking at the meanest flower that blows caused him to think thoughts that lie too deep for tears. Wordsworth also wrote that "Nature never did betray the heart that loved her."

Readers of outdoor writing respect Nature and take her very seriously. But as realists, they know that despite its blessings Nature can also mean floods, forest fires, earthquakes, and hurricanes.

Which brings us to the main point. The job of the outdoor writer is to teach his or her readers all he or she knows about how to cooperate with Nature.

Nature is neither moral nor immoral. She punishes not sin, but carelessness and especially ignorance, which is why outdoor writers are essential to inform people of why and how they must act prudently and effectively to protect the environment.

The source of knowledge for the outdoor writer then is his or her experiences as an observer of Nature and as a practitioner of cooperation with Nature, as a fisherman or hunter, a hiker, mountain climber, bird watcher, pigeon wrangler or farmer.

To these qualifications I would add reading. There is a lot of knowledge about Nature that one will never learn from observation alone, no matter how long he or she lives. But that deficiency can be repaired by reading what others have learned or experienced. My bookcase has many volumes about the outdoors which I have collected over the years. They include *Travels in America* by Peter Kalm, the journal of William Bartram, the *Sand County Almanac* by Aldo Leopold, *Two Little Savages* by Ernest Thompson Seton, and *The Outermost House* by Henry Beston.

But for me the treasure of all outdoor writing is the volume titled *The Compleat Angler or the Contemplative Man's Recreation* by Izaak Walton. He could be a little sentimental about the pleasures of getting off alone in the woods beside a winding brook, wetting a line. But he was also practical. He taught his readers the kind of stream to seek, how to choose bait and how to imprison the bait on the hook.

"If you use a frog for bait," he wrote, "use him as if you loved him. Treat him as carefully as possible that he may live the longer."

For those who want to learn about the craft of outdoor writing there is no better instructor than old Izaak Walton, that kind and gentle man, and his classic book.

Virgil (70 -19 B.C.)

The poems of Virgil which we called the *Georgics* are the first that I know devoted so exclusively to interpreting what the poet saw and felt in a closeness to nature. His epitaph, which he is supposed to have composed said, "I sang of pastures, country, leaders." The word for country he used was "rura," which could be more accurately translated as "country living." And it is in writings about life in the countryside, about wine-grape growing, agriculture and tree planting that he manages to disclose his love of nature. "For thee the field flowers, heavy with tendrils of autumn... nature is manifold in the birth of trees... For some with no human urging come at their own will and spread wide by plain and winding river, like the soft osier and tough broom, the poplar, and pale willow beds with their silvery leafage..."

Virgil lived in the first century before Christ but he is reckoned to have been an inspiration for English poets even into the 19th century.

Sir Francis Bacon (1561-1626)

It is interesting that it was those poets... Browning, Wordsworth, Keats, Shelley and Byron... that were willing to sing of nature, without apologies while the prose writers let nature in by the side door, so to speak, referring to nature while ostensibly pursuing a more practical motive. Sir Francis Bacon, for instance, in his famous essay on gardens, which probably should be given credit for the famous English gardens of today, seemed to be instructing his fellow Englishmen on how to plan a garden that would have certain flowers in bloom through each week of the growing season.

Reverend Gilbert White (1720-1793)

Coming much nearer to our concept of nature writing is the parish priest, Gilbert White, of Selborne, England, born in 1720 who died in 1793. What he wrote he would not have called essays. They were letters describing his detailed and minute observations of nature within his parish. As he said, "All nature is so full that that district produces the most variety that is the most examined." He is described as "the first great English field naturalist." But as his biographer points out, not in the grand manner, "but rather with the simplicity and truth that marks immortality."

He was 46 when he began to write of what he saw in a letter to an understanding friend, a member of the Royal Society. His friends encouraged him to continue his observations and his letter writing which resulted in 1778 in a printed volume entitled *The Natural History and Antiquities of Selborne, in the County of Southhampton*. The book was an immediate success but perhaps characteristic of the attitude towards nature writing at that time, a reviewer complained that there wasn't enough attention given to tillage or agriculture in the parish.

Ralph Waldo Emerson (1803-1882)

This insistence on utilitarianism, on some practical purpose in writings, was the bane of those who would be nature writers right up to Emerson's day.

But the problem did not just go away with Emerson. Biographers of Emerson were intrigued by his comment on his essay on Nature. "I like my book about nature and wish I knew where and how I ought to live," he wrote in his journal. The biographers have made a great deal of that comment, arguing that even at the age of thirty, Emerson had grave doubts about his vocation in life. It was as if he had said, "I like writing about nature but what am I, a grown man, doing writing about this nonutilitarian thing called nature. What good does it do anybody, including me?"

Emerson, it seems, answered his own question in the poem, "The Rhodoro," in which on being asked "Whence is the flower?" he replies, "Beauty is its own excuse for being." For Emerson nature was poetry and self discovery.

Henry David Thoreau (1817-1862)

Henry David Thoreau was not concerned with the doubts that plagued Emerson. Whatever his thoughts, he believed them sufficiently important to put on paper. His emotional identification with nature, with the flora and fauna of Walden Pond, of the Connecticut and Merrimac Rivers, of the Maine woods and Cape Cod, make his journal and essays fascinating reading. Our literature is the richer for Thoreau's having lived and written.

But as a person, I don't find Thoreau compatible. I don't think I would have liked him. His aloofness, his insistence on being a loner, had something of the pathological in it. He was selfish. He was rude and unfeeling toward some who would have been friends. Certainly Emerson befriended him, took him into his home in Concord, encouraged him to write. Emerson could have been hard to take sometimes, and perhaps we shouldn't blame Thoreau for saying in his journal that he was tired of being patronized by Emerson. But Emerson deserved something better, some gracious thanks, for all he did for Thoreau. Thoreau did not shun all company though, while he was writing about the beauty of roughing it in the wilderness of Walden Pond, he would hike every day at noon to his mother's boarding house in Concord to have lunch.

William Bartram (1730-1823)

William Bartram of Philadelphia, following in the footsteps of his father, John Bartram, wrote about nature in the Carolinas, Georgia and Florida. His excuse for so doing was his appointment by King George III to collect and transmit to England samples of plants grown on this continent but unknown in the mother country.

His writings in an edition by Dover, edited by Mark Van Doren, should be available. In any case, a book about the Bartrams was written by Josephine Herbst in the early 1940s.

John Burroughs (1837-1921)

John Burroughs was no doubt one of our most prolific nature writers. I have an 18-volume set of his works, plus his biography of Walt Whitman, but it is his short essay titled "The Adirondacks," that I most admire. He was 26 when with several friends of his own age, he traveled by train from Buttermilk Falls where he taught elementary school to Ticonderoga, from where he hiked across the Boreas River to Grassy Pond and Nate's Pond, about six miles south of Newcomb, and camped at Stillwater. This essay included his description of the white-throat sparrow and its plaintive song. His essay did much, I think, to result in the white-throat's being named the unofficial bird of the Adirondacks.

John Muir (1838-1914)

John Muir is better known in the West than in our parts, and he was, in fact, more of a doer than a writer. But his journal of his walks and his letters and diaries are an important part of America's rich heritage of nature writing. He is given most of the credit for the establishment of the Yosemite and other national parks.

Ernest Thompson Seton (1860 -1946)

Ernest Thompson Seton, who was writing at the turn of the century, was an official naturalist for the government of Manitoba and there was plenty of wildlife around to observe and write about. He wrote *Wild Animals I have Known, Biography of a Grizzly, Trail of the Sandhill Stag*, and of course, *Two Little Savages*, a book that brought a love of the wild into tens of thousands of homes of young people.

Two Little Savages is the story of two boys who spent a summer attempting to live exactly as the Indians lived. They built a teepee. They studied animal tracks and the habits of the wild animals about them. They learned how to make fire by rubbing sticks. And all of their activities were described by Seton, for which this was largely autobiographical, in a way to make young readers conscious of the fulfillment which one can find in nature.

Aldo Leopold (1886-1948)

By the middle of the present century books of nature writing had become relatively abundant. But more and more they were books with a purpose. They had become more scientific, on one hand. On the other hand, their authors were overtly crusading against the tide of development which threatened the existence of wilderness areas through building, and the purity of our environment by pollution.

One of the earliest of these was Aldo Leopold. He was born in Iowa and spent most of his life in the midwest working for state government as a game management expert or ecologist, or teaching in the state universities. In 1934, he was named by President Franklin Roosevelt, along with Jay N. Darling, the cartoonist, and Thomas Beck of *Collier's* magazine, to a special commision to draft plans for the purchase of submarginal farmlands for wildlife habitat. The three worked on the first duck stamp, to establish refuges for migrating ducks and geese along the midwest flyways.

Leopold's classic is the volume of essays and seasonal entries published as *A Sand County Almanac*.

It is a book with a message, the same message Leopold spent his life sending out to any one who would listen. It warned of man's destructive interference in nature's delicate ecological balance and urged upon society a wilderness esthetic that would preserve and protect the environment.

It was first published in 1949, twenty years before we celebrated Earth Day in 1970, and it might well have been the text for the speeches and editorials which hammered at that theme of environmental protection.

But Leopold was more than a crusader. His essays are beautiful descriptions of the seasonal changes in nature. There is in his writings the poetic insight, the serendipity, if that is the word, of the soul-satisfying pleasure we find when we get close to nature.

"Wilderness is the raw material out of which man has hammered the artifact called civilization," he wrote. "No living man will see again the long grass prairie where a sea of prairie flowers lapped at the stirrups of the pioneer... No living man will see again the virgin pineries of the lake states, or the flat woods of the coastal plains of the giant hardwoods..."

Rachel Carson (1907-1964)

If Aldo Leopold was the first nature writer to warn against mankind's destruction of the environment, he was to be followed by another writer, far more influential, with a message so alarming that the course of our history was actually changed.

That writer was Rachel Carson, (1907-1964). In the 1950s she produced two beautiful books, *Under the Sea Wind* and *The Edge of the Sea* which attracted only moderate attention. But in 1962 she published *Silent Spring* which alerted us to the destruction of bird life resulting from the widespread use of DDT and other insecticides.

Nature writers tend to optimism. But it is interesting that Rachel Carson opened her book *Silent Spring* with an uncharacteristic paragrahph from E. B. White:

"I am pessimistic about the human race," wrote White, "Because it is too ingenious for its own good. Our approach to nature is to beat it into submission. We would stand a better chance of survival if we accommodated ourselves to this planet and viewed it appreciatively instead of skeptically and dictatorially."

In any case, following publication of *Silent Spring*, laws were enacted prohibiting use of DDT and certain other highly toxic insecticides. If spring is not silent today, we have Rachel Carson to thank.

Henry Beston

Cape Cod has inspired some of the best nature writing as we have seen from Thoreau's book with that title. It was more than fifty years later that Henry Beston's classic was published, entitled *The Outermost House*.

In this small cabin, he lived for a year on the dunes of Eastham, south of the Coast Guard station, Nausat Light. The Nausat light and the Coast Guard station are still there, but his house was eventually destroyed in an Atlantic storm.

He spent that year as a naturalist, observing, reflecting, and writing. One chapter in the book describes his experience in such a storm.

"When a real nor'easter blows, howling landward through the winter night over a thousand miles of gray tormented seas, all shipping off the Cape must pass the Cape or strand. In the darkness and scream of the storm, in the beat of the endless, icy, crystalline snow, rigging freezes, sails freeze and tear--of a sudden the long booming undertone of the surf sounds under the lee bow--a moment's drift, the feel of the surf twisting the keel of the vessel then the jarring thundering crash and upward drive of the bar."

Beston was fascinated by the idea that standing on the dunes at

Eastham and looking east, there were thousands of miles of ocean, on the other side of which was the old world from which we had come. He had picked the site of his cabin as the most eastern point of our continent. This was the outermost sandpit, the place for the outermost house.

Edwin Way Teale

Most of us know Edwin Way Teale for his books on the seasons . . . *North With The Spring, Autumn Across America,* and *Wandering Through Winter,* published during the 1950s. But a little homework informed me that he was well known as a naturalist in the late 30s. His nature books had won him the John Burroughs medal as a writer of outstanding works in natural history before 1945.

He traveled while he wrote and each of these books has a map and an endpiece. The first one was *North With The Spring,* and he started in Florida while our North Country fields were still white with snow. He said spring traveled north at 16 miles a day, which, if true, would have meant no buds or flowers in the Adirondacks until middle June. Actually we get our redwing blackbirds by middle March and the robins are not far behind. We plant our vegetables around Memorial Day. Spring as we smell it and enjoy it begins as soon as we can feel the warmth of the sun, and the grass greens where patches of snow have melted. But aside from this minor error, Teale's books are very enjoyable. He knew his insects as well as plants.

Joseph Wood Krutch (1893-1970)

Joseph Wood Krutch, like so many good writers, was a Southerner, born in Knoxville, Tennessee in 1893. He died in 1970. He is known most for his works on literature and drama, and for years he was drama critic for *The Nation.* But it should be added that in 1954 he was awarded the John Burroughs medal for excellence in nature writing, which includes three volumes: *The Desert Year*, 1952, *The Best of Two Worlds*, 1953, and *The Twelve Seasons*, 1949.

The opening essay in that collection is entitled "April... The Day of the Peepers:"

"Everyone who has ever visited the country in the spring has heard him trilling from marsh at twilight, and though few have ever caught sight of him, most know that he is a little inch-long frog who has just awakened from his winter's sleep."

William Chapman White (1903-1955)

With William Chapman White, we get closer to home, to Saranac Lake, in fact, to which White and his family retired in 1950. In an introduction to *Just About Everything About the Adirondacks*, Alfred Dashiel, an editor of *Readers Digest* and a lifelong friend, talks about White, first as a fellow student at Princeton and a waiter in the student dining hall. White's first book was about Russia, published in 1930, the product of living with the Russian people and seeing the country not through its government and its ideologues but through the people and their lives.

He began coming to the Adirondacks in 1936 while he wrote for *The New York Times* and *The Herald Tribune*. It was 1950, however, before he made his residence here permanent, and his book *Adirondack Country*, and his essays in *The Herald Tribune*, contain the nature writing that reflected his love of our mountains and valleys, our woods and lakes.

E. B. White (1899-1986)

Some call E. B. White the finest practitioner of the familiar essay in the English language. People love E. B. White, even though they have never met him in the flesh and never will. He wrote with the same intimate quality for which we know Charles Lamb. Our children know him for *Stuart Little* and *Charlotte's Web*. My generation knows him for the relaxed and enjoyable essays in *The New Yorker*, many of which later appeared in collections in books like *The Second Tree From The Corner*, *Quo Vadimus* and *One Man's Meat*.

Early during his career as an editor of *The New Yorker* he bought a farm in Maine and for 40 years, he says, he was dividing his time, half in the city with his editorial responsibilities and half on his Maine farm to which he traveled regularly.

His Maine essays are as much country living as they are nature writing, but there is no contradiction. His essay on the death of a pig has a breath of country air about it and the reader can smell the scent of lilacs along with the musty odor of the pig sty. *A Report on Spring* is not only about the season. He buys a puppy and takes him along to the farm in May where he finds that mice have eaten his flowers, his pear tree has bark trouble and his white-faced steer has warts on his neck. But in broad daylight a raccoon appears and the rest of the essay is about the coon.

White was born in 1899 in Mt. Vernon, New York and died in 1986. He has left us a rich heritage of delightful reading matter.

The garden club ladies have a similar feeling about his wife, Katherine, whose books on growing flowers are on the library shelves.

Stephen Jay Gould

One of the most interesting writers today is Stephen Jay Gould, a professor of science history at Harvard, whose essay appears each month in Natural History, the publication of the American Museum of Natural History.

Professor Gould would call himself a writer of natural history rather than of nature. His essays illustrate how nature writing as we know it from the past has turned more and more to the explicitly scientific. This should not surprise us. What has always attracted us to reading about nature is our curiosity. We have a fascination about the life around us, the life of the animal and plant world, the stars and the planets.

In *The Panda's Thumb*, a collection of his essays from natural History, he begins with a quotation from Pliny about 79 AD:

"Nature is to be found in her entirety nowhere more than in her smallest creatures."

Both volumes reflect his fascination with evolution. They constitute a defense of Charles Darwin, but they are more than that. They are an effort to understand how natural selection and the survival of the fittest operated over millions of years to produce the vast majority of life now existing.

I find it interesting that flowering plants appeared first 136 million years ago; conifers and ferns and mosses between 400 and 240 million years ago. But most striking is the Cambrian explosion 500 million years ago when insects, worms, spiders, octopi, fish, reptiles and birds made their appearance.

What I think Professor Gould contributed to our understanding of evolution is that it did not develop in a steady straight line of progress, but jumped forward at times, slowed down, even stopped, and then made new bursts ahead. All of these developments were not necessarily useful, such as the panda's thumb, or the hen's teeth or the horse's toe. They were appendages like our appendix which so far as we know played no useful role, yet did not interfere seriously with the evolutionary development of the organism.

Professor Gould made a study of the so-called intelligence tests which were exploited to promote laws against immigration from southern and eastern Europe, Asia and Africa.

Recently in my own correspondence with Professor Gould, in drawing upon my own experience to confirm something he had written on this subject, I cited the number of young people in our towns, children of parents who had never been to college or who may have never finished high school, who were off to college that year.

His letter to me bears on that subject: "One needn't only look to accomplishments of young people in your area to prove the theses of flexibility in human potential. Just look at all the nations deemed inherently ineducable by the army mental tests of World War I -- virtually all countries of southern and eastern Europe. Their grandchildren today are indistinguishable from the offspring of the oldest Yankees."

I suppose a good example of what he is saying are Governor Cuomo and Vice Presidential candidate Geraldine Ferraro, both Italian-Americans whose parents came from southern Europe.

This may seem a far cry from nature writing but it isn't. Professor Gould's essays are beautifully written and induce upon the reader a mood of quiet enjoyment, all the more gratifying because they are provocative, they make one think, and they provide information.

Professor Gould is young--only about 45--and while suffering from a terminal cancer, he is continuing his teaching, his studies, and his writing.

Dr. Lewis Thomas

It is not easy to fit Dr. Lewis Thomas into any category, let alone that of a nature essayist of great charm. He has published his essays in the *New England Journal of Medicine*, an unlikely place, one would think, for brief, effortless pieces which partake of the language of poetry. Joyce Carol Oates reviewing his first collection, entitled *Lives of the Cell*, said the 29 essays in the little volume were "masterpieces in the art of the essay."

They are certainly more science than nature, but the true lover of nature inevitably turns to science. Dr. Thomas calls himself a biology watcher.

Since *Lives of the Cell* was published in 1974, three other volumes have followed: *The Medusa and the Snail*; *Late Night Thoughts on*

Listening to Mahler's Symphony, and another whose title I have forgotten, about the most significant breakthrough in the practice of medicine.

Dr. Thomas looks at the cell, finds it exciting; sees the human organism as an organized collection of cells and ponders whether an infinite being looking at our planet might see it, the planet, as similarly a collection of cells in a great unit.

But for a biology watcher, Dr. Thomas is also a watcher of less clinical matters. He describes a house cat with a mouse in her mouth and immediately explains the work of something called endorphs which are released by the organism to reduce pain to nothing, or even to euphoria. The human body also has this capacity, he says, and suggests that is what Montaigne, the famous French essayist, had in mind when he described the expression of peace and contentment on the face of a dying friend.

More in the tradition of the nature writer is one essay I have in mind, named "The Music of the Spheres." He tells us about how termites make percussive sounds by beating their heads against the floor, how bats sense their surroundings by their sonar instruments; how prairie hens, rabbits and mice make drumming sounds; how beetles tick by pressing a part of their abdomen to the ground; how gorillas beat their chests; how rattlesnakes rattle, and so on. He suggests that the urge humans have to create music such as the Brandenberg Concertos is similar to those of the creatures to which he has listened. And of course, characteristically, he goes on to wonder what a visitor from outer space might make of our sounds on this planet.

DiNunzio and Lacy

A few words on a very recent book of nature writing. It is called the *Adirondack Wildguide,* written by Michael G. DiNunzio and illustrated by Anne E. Lacy. Whereas the Reverend Gilbert White examined nature within one small parish, Mike and Anne have examined it within the six million acreage of the Adirondack Park.

The writing, and the drawings and the paintings were done at the Hand House in Elizabethtown over two years sponsored by the Adirondack Nature Conservancy and the Adirondack Council.

It is, as the subtitle says, a natural history of the Adirondack Park beautifully written and beautifully illustrated, including some exciting photographs by Gary Randorf.

From the cover you can get an excellent thumbnail description of its contents:

"It takes you through the wildlands of the Adirondack with an ecologist as your guide. Forests, fields, streams and mountain tops will be seen from a fresh perspective. Interrelationships between plants and animals and their environment are explained and illustrated in an informative entertaining manner."

Other Almanacs

It is time to put aside the *Old Farmer's Almanac* of last year and turn to its successor, which is more of a ritual than a necessity. We have little need of the almanacs in these days when our weather information comes readily from television and radio. We were early apprised that the solstice arrived at 5:51 PM on December 21, providing the shortest day of the year. But it was from the almanac we learned that daylight was nine hours and four minutes, that daylight would lengthen on an average of a minute a day until the equinox about noon March 20.

Thus the boundary which technically marks the beginning and end of winter.

The weather forecasts of the almanacs were considered important by our agrarian ancestors who must have suffered considerably when the long-term forecasts were wrong. Now long-term weather forecasting has so benefitted from science and its instruments that at least in broad terms we can expect what we get. For instance, Ray Falconer, at the Atmospheric Sciences Research Center in Albany advises us that the bulk of this winter's snow will have fallen by the end of December and that the rest of the winter will bring below average snowfall. We have a lot of confidence in Mr. Falconer, and so has Barney Fowler of the *Albany Times-Union* who says he has learned from experience that "if Ray Falconer leaves the party early," so does he.

The most famous American almanac was that established by Benjamin Franklin in Philadephia in 1733 under the pseudonym of Richard Saunders, and known as *Poor Richard's Almanac*. There was already an almanac in that city published by Titan Leeds and Franklin anticipated tough competition. His solution to that problem was to report to his readers that his competitor, Mr. Leeds, had died. But Titan failed to appreciate the humor and replied that this was "a gross falsehood."

Franklin continued his annual little essay on Leeds until 1739 when Leeds did actually die. In that issue of his almanac, Franklin insisted he had a letter Leeds had written him beyond the grave in which he acknowledges that Poor Richard had accurately dated his death. The ghost of Leeds said his *Almanac* had been published by imposters who operated entirely without any knowledge of the Planets Motions, etc. "So that the Stuff they publish as an Almanack in my Name is no more mine than yours."

ABOUT THE AUTHOR

Rob Hall was editor and publisher of a weekly newspaper in New York's North Country from 1958 until 1971. During that time, he served as a member of Governor Rockefeller's Temporary Commission to Study the Future of the Adirondacks, and he founded *Adirondack Life* magazine. From 1971 to 1976, he was editor of *New York's Conservationist* magazine. During this time the magazine cited as the best conservation magazine in the United States by the American Association of Conservation Information. A previous book of his essays was *The Empty Nest.*

Mr. Hall continues to write weekly editorials for upstate New York publications. As a popular columnist, he writes authoritatively about local, national, and international politics. But his great love and source of inspiration for all his writing, including the political, is nature as he has studied it in the Adirondacks for over thirty years.